Interactive

Dictations

Books by Judy DeFilippo and Catherine Sadow:

Basic Dictations • photocopyable text and CD
Beginner
Great Dictations • text and CD
High-Beginner to Low-Intermediate
Interactive Dictations • text and CD
Low-Intermediate to Intermediate
Dictations for Discussion • text and 2 CD's
Intermediate to Advanced

by Jane Gragg Lewis:

Dictation Riddles • photocopyable text and 4 CD's
Beginner to Advanced

by Edgar Sather, Catherine Sadow, and George Draper:

People at Work • text, teacher's book, and 3 CD's
Listening and Communicative Skills
Interviews with ten people in the workplace
Intermediate to Advanced

Interactive Dictations

A Listening/Speaking/Writing Text
Second, Revised Edition

Judy DeFilippo
Catherine Sadow

PRO LINGUA  ASSOCIATES

Pro Lingua Associates, Publishers
P.O. Box 1348
Brattleboro, Vermont 05302 USA
Office: 802 257 7779
Orders: 800 366 4775
Email: info@ProLinguaAssociates.com
WebStore www.ProLinguaAssociates.com
SAN: 216-0579

*At **Pro Lingua***
our objective is to foster an approach
to learning and teaching that we call
***interplay,** the **inter**action of language*
learners and teachers with their materials,
with the language and culture,
and with each other in active,
creative, and productive
***play**.*

ISBN 13: 978-0-86647-357-6; 10: 0-86647-357-2
      Audio CD ISBN 13: 978-0-86647-358-3; 10: 0-86647-358-0
      Text/CD Set ISBN 13: 978-0-86647-359-0; 10: 0-86647-359-9

Interactive Dictations was designed by Arthur A. Burrows. It was set in Palatino, the most widely used, and pirated, face of the twentieth century, which was designed by Hermann Zapf in 1948 in Frankfurt. Although modern, it is based on Renaissance designs typical of the Palatinate area in Germany. The illustrated proverb on page 114 is © 2002 by Patrick R. Moran from *Lexicarry*. Many of the illustrations in this book are from The Big Box of Art, Copyright © Hemera Technologies Inc. and Art Explosion 750,000 Images, Copyright © Nova Development Corporation. Other photographs are from Dreamstime Agency: p. xvi © Monkey Business Images, p. 3 © Scott Griessel, p. 14 Ron Sumners, p. 13 © Parick Hardin, p. 20 © Zurijeta, p. 23 © Karen Struthers, p. 25 © Monkey Business Images, p. 30 © Jaboardm, p. 31 © Christos Georghiou, p. 34 & 37 © Monkey Business Images, p. 41 © Americanspirit, p. 43 © Nzmphotoworks, p. 45 © Raymond Gregory, p. 47 © Robert Kneschke, p. 49 © Sbukley, p. 50 © Juri Samsonov, p. 56 © Stanimir Ivanov, p. 58 © Americanspirit, p. 70 © Wishedauan, p. 77 © Nikolay Mamluk, , p. 80 © Dprewitt, p. 87 © Libya + Media, p. 95 © Auntpittypat, p, 97 © Patrick Hermans, p. 98 © Nolte Lourens, p. 100 © Monkey Business Images, p. 102 © David Watts Jr, p. 106 © Matthew Clausen, p. 107 © Hongqi Zhang, p. 110 © Featureflash, p.113 © Serrnovik, p. 125 Fasphotographic, p. 129 © Kenneth Sponsler, p. 130 © Diana Valujeva. p. 135 © Robyn Mackenzie, p. 138 © 144@Pasco06, p. 147 © Hongqi Zhang, p. 150 © Featureflash. Cover photo – Vermont lake: Songquan Deng. The book was printed and bound by Gasch Printing in Odenton, Maryland.

Printed in the United States of America
Second, Revised Edition, fourth printing 2018. 3200 copies in print.

Contents

Contents ❀

❀ *Acknowledgements* ❀

The authors based many of their activities on concepts introduced by P. Davis and M. Rinvolucri, who co-authored *Dictation, New Methods, New Possibilities*, Cambridge University Press, 1988.

The authors are grateful to the authors, publishers, and others who have given permission to reprint copyrighted materials:

The Academy of Achievement: Amy Tan interview
http//www.achievement.org
Cartoon Stock: *Chocoholics*
The Hingham Journal: *The Noblest of Professions* by Cathy Conley
The Boston Globe: *Eat that Insect?* by Jessica Kowal
The New York Times: *How Honest Are You?* by N. Onishi
The Chicago Tribune: *Dear Amy* by A. Dickinson
Anonymous Internet Sources
Privacy
Dear Mom and Dad
Made ... Where?
John and Mary to D.C. by B. F. Swartz

The authors wish to thank the following teachers who field-tested the text and gave valuable feedback:

Daniel Doherty, Immigrant Learning Center, Malden, MA
Shirley Taylor, SCALE, Somerville, MA
Laura Brooks, SCALE, Somerville, MA
Liz Nicholson, Showa Boston Institute
Debby Fitzpatrick, Showa Boston Institute
Kathrine Douthit, Showa Boston Institute

For our grandchildren

Courtney
Connor
Eli
Zachary

Introduction

Interactive Dictations is a low-intermediate to intermediate level text that is intended to improve the listening, speaking, and writing skills of ESL students. Reading skills are also reinforced, along with attention to vocabulary and grammar. This text provides a wide variety of dictations that include provocative news items, problems to solve, and decisions to make. Each dictation naturally leads to a discussion activity that can take twenty to thirty minutes.

Teachers can pick and choose which dictations meet the needs, interests, and levels of their particular students. Dictations are classified by topic, but one topic is not necessarily easier or harder than another. Topics can be used to supplement a theme or grammar point of an existing text.

Within topics, the units are designed to stand alone — each unit contains one dictation activity, a follow-up discussion, and a writing activity. Pair or small-group work is encouraged in both the dictation and discussion sections. This text includes several cooperative learning activities.

Some units are short. Teachers can use these as fill-ins for a 15 to 30 minute lesson. Longer units will take 30 to 60 minutes.

The full dictations are available in the second part of the book. A CD with the full dictations is also available.

❀ Different Types of Dictation ❀

Dictation has been presented in many forms through the years in reading, listening, grammar, and writing classes. It is also used as an assessment procedure. This text, however, does not deal with scoring or analyzing student work. The dictations are meant to be a challenging springboard to discussion and writing by which the students are encouraged to use the language they have just encountered in the dictation.

This text includes four forms of dictation: **partial, pair, dictogloss,** and **prediction.** While all units include pair and group work in the discussion segments, several units will include more extensive cooperative and role-play types of activities. See the unit on proverbs as an example.

Partial (sometimes known as *cloze*)

Most of the dictations in this text are partial dictations where words, phrases, or chunks of language have been deleted, and students are required to listen and write down the missing words. All the dictations should be discussed upon completion. Pair work is encouraged.

Pair (sometimes known as mutual)

This dictation requires students to work in pairs to combine two-part texts into one continuous piece. One student has a copy of dictation "Student A," and the other has dictation "Student B." Each student has half of the text. They should not look at each other's sheets. Student A dictates and Student B writes, then B dictates and A writes, and so on until the story is complete.

Dictogloss

In this kind of dictation, the focus is on getting the gist or main idea of a sentence or short paragraph.

There are many variations of the dictogloss technique. In the directions for the sentence-level dictogloss, students are told that they will hear a sentence only once, after which they are to jot down the words they can recall and try to reconstruct the sentence in writing as accurately as they can. The first time this is done, the teacher will probably have to allow the students a second reading until they discover that they need to pay attention the first time around. As the students work at rebuilding the sentence, they can work in pairs and then fours.

Prediction

Prediction lessons come in two parts. The first part focuses more on reading skills and grammar. The students are required to work in pairs, reading the passage and predicting (or guessing) what should be in each blank space. Any logical or grammatically correct word or phrase can be accepted. Part Two requires the students to listen to the same passage and see if their guesses were correct, or similar.

❀ **Tips for Teachers** ❀

1. When reading the full dictations, try to speak naturally, at normal speed, keeping the features of the spoken language. If you are reading the full text at normal speed and you know the exercise will be fairly easy for your students, give the word, phrase, or chunk of language only once. Try to start with a pace that is comfortable for your students, and then make them work a bit at understanding. If you think the text will be difficult for your students, repeat two, possibly three times. When field testing our material, several teachers said that they thought the material looked quite difficult for their students, but they were surprised how well their students did. It's up to you to decide what works best. If you have to repeat more than three times, the text is too difficult for your students.

2. The students may want to check the spelling of a word or words as you are giving the dictation. It's best to tell them to wait until the end of the activity.

3. For numbers, have the students write numerals, rather than the word (15, instead of fifteen), except for single-digit numbers (1-9). They should also use dollar ($) and percentage (%) symbols rather than writing out the words.

4. One key to making the dictation a positive experience is to have students correct their own work. When the dictation is completed, the students check with each other in pairs on what they've heard, while you walk around helping and clarifying. This, in itself, allows for a great deal of discussion. After they have self-corrected, they can turn to the full dictation texts for confirmation. You can then go over the dictation with the class and discuss whatever vocabulary or concepts they don't understand.

5. Rather than read the full dictations from the appendix, you may find it helpful to copy the page you're dictating and fill in the blanks yourself ahead of time. This is useful when giving feedback. It's easier when you're working from the same page as your students. Here is an example from "Proverbs":

    1. There's no *place like home.*

    2. Don't *count your chickens* before they are hatched.

6. There was no one pattern that was followed when choosing words or phrases to be deleted. Sometimes the deletions focus on idioms, sometimes on numbers, sometimes grammar, sometimes vocabulary.

7. *Interactive Dictations* also works well for substitute teachers, since a minimum amount of preparation is needed.

8. You and your students can also create dictations from local newspapers, the Internet, or any other source. This way you can choose a timely topic and easily adapt it to the level of your students.

9. With higher-level students, you may want to ask a student to read a full dictation. The reader may prepare for this by listening to the CD.

10. Discussions. The discussions can be by pairs, small groups, or the entire class.

11. Cooperative activities have been included in four of the units. These are extensions of pair and group work and they are one of the best ways to have everyone in the class very involved.

Day 1. There are four groups, A,B,C, and D. On Day 1, everyone in each group is responsible for researching part of the material assigned to that group.

Day 2. All groups reassemble, and the group members go over all the information they have gathered, being sure that each member is fully familiar with all the material.

Day 2 or 3. New groups are formed. Each group includes one person from each of the original groups. In other words, each new group will consist of one A, one B, one C, and one D. The Group A person is responsible for sharing all of the Group A material. By the end of this activity every member of the class should have the complete information. This can be a lengthy activity, but it is very valuable, especially for shyer students.

❀ Using the CD ❀

Although it is not necessary to have and use the accompanying CD, many teachers find that having the CD provides greater flexibility in using the material. It can be used in several ways:

1. Play the track once through without stopping **before** reading the dictation to the students. This will introduce the topic and give the students a head start toward comprehending the dictation when it is read to them. Playing the recording before the dictation also provides excellent listening comprehension practice, valuable preparation for listening to lectures.

2. To give the students a chance to hear a different voice, have the students take the dictation from the CD. Although more challenging, this can help the students prepare for standardized listening tests. You can use the pause button; that will allow the students time to fill in the blanks.

3. Play the CD **after** the students have taken the dictation and checked their answers. This can help the students improve and become more confident in listening comprehension.

Teachers suggest that varying the way the recordings are used from unit to unit interests their students and gives their classes the opportunity to express their preferences.

On the CD, each dictation text is on a separate track. The CD track numbers are given in the table of contents of this book (v-vi), and also next to the titles of the gapped texts (1-112) and the titles of full dictations texts (113-151).

❀ Using a Listening Laboratory ❀

Almost any dictation that is done in class can also be done in the language lab. However, there are some additional things that can be done in the lab that cannot be done in the classroom.

1. Read a short partial dictation in the lab. Then have the students tape what they have written. You can collect both, and then on the student tape give some feedback on their pronunciation.

2. The students create their own partial dictation and make four or five copies of it. They record it carefully and leave the results at their stations. They then move from station to station doing four or five of each other's dictations. The students' dictations can follow a general theme – food, for example – or a specific form – a joke or poem.

3. Dictate a chunk of language. The students listen and record it. Add another chunk. The students record again. At the end of the short, fairly simple dictation, the students transcribe it. Collect their transcriptions and make appropriate comments and corrections.

4. Dictate a problem. An example might be a "Dear Abby" letter that you have turned into a dictation. After each student has done the dictation, they record the solution to the problem. You should listen and respond to the solution, or the students can move from station to station listening to their fellow students and making comments of agreement or disagreement. By preparing short, easy-to-understand dictations first, you can also use this technique to introduce current political or social topics that you think will be of particular interest to your students.

❀ **Pronunciation** ❀

Students are often familiar with a word, and they may read it easily, attempt to write it, but still hesitate to use it orally because they don't know how to pronounce it.

Consequently, teachers should pronounce the words in the vocabulary list and have students repeat the words aloud. Students may then be encouraged to use some of the words in the discussion with their partner.

❀ **About the Full Dictation Texts** ❀

The complete texts of the dictations begin on page 113. You can read these full texts to give the dictations, have a student read them, or use the CD.

Interactive Dictations

Proverbs

Introduction ❄

full text on page 113 (cd track 1)

A proverb is a short, popular saying that expresses some common truth or thought. Every culture has them. Here are a few American ones. After you have talked about these three, share one proverb that you know with the class.

1. A picture is worth a thousand words.
2. When the cat's away, the mice will play.
3. An apple a day keeps the doctor away.

Vocabulary and Pronunciation ❄
1. **to hatch -** to come out of an egg; be born
2. **to spoil -** to make bad or rotten
3. **a broth -** a clear soup
4. **a trick -** an action animals are trained to do
5. **a worm -** a small crawling animal with no legs
6. **hard -** difficult

Partial Dictation ❄

Fill in the blank spaces. Correct and discuss the meaning of each proverb with a partner.

1. There's no _____ _____ _____.

2. Don't _____ _____ _____ before they're hatched.

3. First _____, first _____.

4. Love makes the world _____ _____.

5. _____ is _____.

6. _____ _____ _____ spoil the broth.

7. You can't _____ _____ _____ _____ new tricks.

8. You can't have your cake and _____ _____ _____.

9. _____ and _____.

10. The _____ _____ catches the worm.

11. The _____ _____ is the hardest.

12. The apple doesn't _____ _____ _____ from the tree.

Discussion ❋

Share two proverbs that you know with a partner and explain what they mean.

    1.

    2.

Cooperative Learning ❋

Work in four groups with 3, 4, or 5 students in each group. Each student finds answers to one or several proverbs and reports back to their group. Then all four groups share the answers they have found in reconfigured groups, each person responsible for all of the answers from their group.

Group One

    1. Beauty is only skin deep.
    2. Many hands make light work.
    3. Opportunity seldom knocks twice.
    4. The grass is always greener in the other person's yard.
    5. The squeaky wheel gets the oil.

Group Two

    1. Two heads are better than one.
    2. One man's loss is another man's gain.
    3. Life is just a bowl of cherries.
    4. Let sleeping dogs lie.
    5. It never rains but it pours.

Group Three

    1. Don't put off until tomorrow what you can do today.
    2. The love of money is the root of all evil.
    3. All work and no play makes Jack a dull boy.
    4. Don't put all your eggs in one basket.
    5. To err is human, to forgive, divine.

Group Four

    1. People who live in glass houses shouldn't throw stones.
    2. Honesty is the best policy.
    3. You don't get something for nothing.
    4. A stitch in time saves nine.
    5. Do unto others as you would have them do unto you.

Writing ❄

Choose a proverb that you know and write a short paragraph about it. If possible, include a personal experience in your writing.

If you prefer, write about one of these proverbs:

(from Africa): It takes a village to raise a child.

(from China): There are always ears on the other side of the wall.

Optimists and Pessimists

Introduction ❋

full text on page 114 (cd track 2)

Are you an optimist or a pessimist?

Vocabulary and Pronunciation ❋

1. **gas guzzlers** - cars that "eat up" or use more gasoline than necessary
2. **strict** - expecting rules to be followed; stern
3. **suspenseful** - full of nervous uncertainty
4. **food poisoning** - a stomach illness caused by eating bad food
5. **weird** - strange or unusual
6. **an optimist** - one who sees things positively
7. **a pessimist** - one who sees things negatively

Partial Dictation ❋

Listen and write the words you hear in the blank spaces. Then, with a partner, decide on a response to these complainers. Take the optimist's (or positive) view.

Example:
(complaint) "The winters here in the Northeast are very cold."
(response)   That's true, but you can go skating and enjoy the quiet beauty of the first snowfall.

1. "The food at McDonald's _____ _____ _____.

    On the other hand, _____.

2. " _____ _____ is illogical."

    OK, but _____.

3. "There are ____ _____ _____ in the U.S."

    That's true, but _____.

4. "It's been raining for _____ _____ _____."

    Yes, but _____.

5. "American cars _____ _____ _____."

    I know, but _____.

6. "I have to pay a lot _____ _____ _____."

    Anyway, _____.

7. "My parents _____ _____ _____."

    That may be true, but_____.

Discussion and Pairwork ❋

You're walking down a busy street behind a young woman (YW) with a cell phone. You can hear only her part of the conversation, of course. Can you guess what the other person (OP) is saying? Work with a partner and decide how to complete the conversation. Then share your conversations with the class.

1. Conversation One

YW: I just had lunch at that new Italian restaurant in the North End. It was terrible!

OP: _____.

YW: I tried the chicken parmesan and the chicken wasn't cooked enough. It was pink.

OP: _____.

YW: Right. I'm just glad I didn't end up in the hospital with food poisoning.

2. Conversation Two

YW: You know that teller's job I interviewed for at City Bank? Well, I didn't get it.

OP: _____.

YW: Well, the woman who interviewed me was really weird.

OP: _____.

YW: She asked me if I liked money.

OP: Really? _____.

3. Conversation Three

YW: That used car I just bought is making strange noises.

OP: _____.

YW: I did, but my mechanic couldn't find any problems.

OP: _____.

YW: Yeah, that's a good idea.

Discussion ❋

Here are some situations where people should turn off their cell phones. Work with a partner and talk about whether you have experienced these situations. Share your experiences with the class.

Part A

1. You are in a funeral home and the minister is saying a prayer for the deceased. A cell phone rings.
2. You are in the middle of an important exam. A cell phone rings.
3. You are watching a suspenseful movie in a theater. A cell phone rings.

Part B

Who's the complainer? With a partner, decide who is complaining. In some cases there is more than one possible answer.

Example: "Why don't you do the laundry this week, dear?"   Wife (to husband)

1. "This bedroom is always such a mess."   _____
2. "This car I just got is a lemon."   _____
3. "She's always wearing my clothes without permission."   _____
4. "He promised not to raise taxes and then he did."   _____
5. "The people upstairs are so noisy."   _____
6. "You really should lose 50 pounds."   _____
7. "I want everyone to be on time for class tomorrow."   _____

Idioms

Here are some common idioms or expressions that you hear when people are upset. Can you guess what they mean?

1. Get off my back!
2. He gave me the run around.
3. I don't like being cooped up in an office all day.
4. He gets on my nerves.
5. I'm fed up with the situation.
6. Those kids drive me crazy! They're driving me out of my mind.
7. Mary got up on the wrong side of the bed this morning.

Writing

Today you can be an optimist or a pessimist. Write a paragraph about a good or bad experience you had and explain what you learned from this experience. Begin with an introductory sentence and then explain step by step what happened.

Brain Teasers!

full text on page 115 (cd track 3)

Introduction ❋

Here are some tricky questions. Don't be fooled! But don't worry, you won't look foolish!

Vocabulary and Pronunciation ❋

1. **feathers** - birds' "clothing"
2. **cement** - a material that, when mixed with water, will harden like a rock
3. **a pound** - a weight of 16 ounces or 453.6 grams
4. **to bury** - put in the ground after death
5. **a sand pile** - a little hill children make with the sand at the beach
6. **a lion** - the largest wild cat
7. **a tiger** - a wild, striped cat
8. **to attack** - to use violent force

Partial Dictation and Discussion ❋

After checking the dictation, try to figure out the answer with a partner.

Example: When the Vice-President of the U.S. dies, who is the President?
Answer: The President!

1. Which is heavier, a pound of feathers, or a _____ _____ _____ ?

2. How many _____ _____ does the average person have?

3. Can a man _____ _____ _____ in northern United States be buried in Canada?

4. A little girl is playing _____ _____ _____. She is making sand piles. She has

   _____ _____ in one place and _____ _____ in another place.

   If she puts them _____ _____, how many sand piles will she have?

5. Bob _____ _____ _____ Sam. Sam is standing behind Bob at

   the _____ _____. How is that possible?

6. _____ _____ _____ have a lion attack you or a tiger?

7. What word, if pronounced right, _____ _____ but if pronounced "wrong" _____

   _____ ?

8. Do you know the thing that has keys that open _____ _____, has space but _____

   _____, and allows you to enter but _____ _____ _____ ?

Riddles ❋ *(cover column B first and try to guess)*

A

1. Why do birds fly south for the winter?

2. What kind of water never freezes?

3. Who did Burger King marry?

4. Where can you always find money?

B

d. in a dictionary

c. Dairy Queen

b. hot water

a. it's too far to walk

Writing ❋ *Write five riddles and share them with the class.*

Trivia Contest

Introduction ❋

full text on page 116 (cd track 4)

Trivia is information that is not important but is fun to know.

Vocabulary and Pronunciation ❋

1. **an abbreviation** - shortened form of a word or phrase
2. **a license plate** - a permit from the government attached to a car in the form of
   a piece of metal with numbers and letters on it.

Partial Dictation ❋

After you fill in the blank spaces, work together in pairs or small groups and answer as many questions as you can. The group with the most correct answers wins the contest.

1. What does the abbreviation ET _____ _____ ?

2. What do people put _____, _____, and _____ dressing on?

3. What is the _____ _____ ____ _____ that a woman has had at one time?

4. What do people in the United States have to do ____ _____ ____ ?

5. What is the name of the _____ _____ _____ in India ?

6. What do you do when you _____ ____ _____ ?

7. Who wrote ____ _____ _____ ?

8. What sports event takes place ____ ____ _____ ?

9. Which is the _____ _____ ?

10. What _____ do they speak in _____ ?

11. What is present in _____, _____, _____, and chocolate ?

12. What was the _____ _____ _____ and where ____ ____ _____ ?

13. Who does a car with the _____ ____ on the license plate _____ ____ ?

14. Who was both _____ and _____, but became a _____ ?

Cooperative Learning ❊

Work in four groups with an equal number of students in each group. Below are four sets of trivia questions, and each group is assigned one of these sets. Each person in the group finds out the answers to one or more of the trivia questions and then reports back to their group. This can be done as homework or in class. Each person in the group must be prepared to explain the answers to all the questions in their set. Then all the people are reassigned to newly configured groups. Finally each person shares with their new group the answers to their set of questions.

Set One

1. What is the coldest month in the US?
2. What are "subs," "po boys," and "hoagies" ?
3. What's the hardest rock?
4. Where is the smallest bone in the human body?
5. Who wrote *Julius Caesar, Macbeth,* and *Hamlet?*

Set Two

1. What is the most popular spectator sport in the world?
2. What does the modern slang word "cool" really mean?
3. End this common phrase, "See you later, ...
4. What first language is spoken by the most people in the world?
5. How can you write the words "I scream" so that they have a different meaning?

Set Three

1. How many events are there in the decathlon?
2. What are "soda" and "pop" common words for?
3. What book has been translated into the most languages?
4. What is the full term for e-mail?
5. How many words are there in the English language?

Set Four

1. What insect has been around since the time of the dinosaur?
2. What do "bucks," "fins," and "C notes" refer to?
3. What does UFO stand for?
4. What was the previous name of Thailand?
5. How many is a "baker's dozen"?

Writing ❋ *In a group, write a mini trivia contest (5 questions) for your classmates.*

1.

2.

3.

4.

5.

Chocoholics, Unite!

full text on page 117 (cd track 5)

Introduction ❖

"Hi, my name is Eleanor and I am addicted to chocolate. I think about chocolate always, except when I'm asleep and then I dream about chocolate!"

"In the beginning there was a word, and the word was chocolate, and it was good."

Vocabulary and Pronunciation ❖

1. **to crave -** to desire greatly; to need right away
2. **a mood -** an emotional state
3. **an addict -** a person physically or emotionally dependent on a substance
4. **currency -** the money used to pay for goods and services
5. **sinful -** against religious ideas of what is right

"there is but one path to the inner peace you seek. — chocolate!

Partial Dictation ❖

After you have filled in the words, work with a partner and decide if the statements are fact or opinion. Write F for fact and O for opinion.

___ 1. Chocolate from Belgium ____ _____ _____.

___ 2. People crave chocolate more than _____ _____ _____.

___ 3. Chocolate _____ ___ _____ associated with mood, emotion, and addiction.

___ 4. Chocolate is sinful because it has lots of _____ _____ _____.

___ 5. Chocolate lovers _____ _____ _____ for almost 3000 years.

___ 6. Chocolate comes from cacao beans, and ____ _____ _____ was used as a form of currency.

___ 7. _____ _____ _____ cacao trees in Africa, Southeast Asia, and in South and Central America.

___ 8. You can _____ _____ _____ when you are depressed or stressed.

Discussion ❖

Part A. With a partner, talk about these addictions. Do you have one or know someone who does? Explain! Can you add some to the list?
1. shopaholic
2. netaholic
3. chocoholic
4. TV addict
5. soda addict
6. smoker
7. alcoholic
8. drug addict
9. workaholic

Part B. Talk about the meanings of these "addiction" idioms and expressions with the class.
1. Cigarettes run his life.
2. She can't kick the habit.
3. I'm hooked on the Internet.
4. She needs a fix.
5. He's having a nicotine fit.
6. You got a buzz from the drink.
7. I shop till I drop.

Writing ❖

Pretend there is someone you know who is hooked on shopping. Write a letter to them and give suggestions that will help this person kick the habit. Before you write, talk about the letter with a partner.

Dear _____,
(friend's name)

Your friend,

_____
(your name)

What Do You Eat?

full text on page 118 (cd track 6)

Introduction ♣

A recent poll gives us a look at when we eat, where we eat, what we eat, and how often we eat. Do you eat breakfast? Where do you eat it, and what do you eat?

Vocabulary and Pronunciation ♣

1. **two-thirds** - 2/3 (66.666%)
2. **three-fourths** - 3/4 (75%)
3. **two out of three** - another way of saying two thirds
4. **a snack** - food that is eaten between meals
5. **a slice** - a thin piece cut from a larger piece, for example, a slice of bread
6. **to nibble** - to eat a little or with small quick bites
7. **prime time** - the time of night when more people watch television

Partial Dictation ❖

Listen and write the words you hear in the blank spaces. Correct and discuss with a partner.

Breakfast. During the work week, _____-_____ of Americans eat breakfast, _____- _____ of them at home. About _____ ____ _____ eats breakfast at work: _____ ___ _____while driving or commuting. The most popular breakfast is _____ or _____ cereal (67%), followed by _____, or muffins, or bagels (___ ___), and eggs (___ ___). _____-_____ also snack on cereal, and _____ _____ admit they eat cereal for dinner ... sometimes.

Weekends. On _____ and Sunday, _____ _____ of us eat breakfast at home. Eggs are the _____ Sunday breakfast for more than _____. Bacon, ham, or sausages are nearly as _____; so are pancakes or waffles.

Lunch. Sandwiches _____ _____ at midday. _____ in _____ of us put our food between two _____ of bread. _____ ___ _____ eats _____ _____.

Dinner. About _____ ___ _____ who bring home _____ food said they prefer everything ready-to-eat, rather than also having a side dish prepared at home. _____ is the favorite food-to-go (the choice of _____ _____), followed by _____ food (___ ___) and _____ _____ such as hamburgers or tacos (_____ _____).

Snacks. Evening is _____ _____ for snackers. Nearly _____-_____ of Americans snack after dinner (_____ in front of the ____), and _____ ____ nibble all day long.

Discussion ❖ *Discuss these questions with a partner. Then share your ideas with the class.*

1. Based on this dictation and your own experience, do you think Americans eat well?
2. Has your way of eating changed recently? How?
3. What are some of the foods that are new to you that you like?
4. What are some of the foods you grew up with that Americans don't know about?

Discussion ♣ *Discuss these questions with a partner. Then share your ideas with the class.*

It's 9:00 p.m. You decide that you're hungry and you want a snack. Below are some foods that you can choose from. Which of the following do you think are the three healthiest snacks to have? Which three are the unhealthiest? Which do you think you personally would choose and why?

a small box of raisins	a package of three Oreo cookies
a large apple	a bowl of Cheerios and milk
a small bag of potato chips	a bowl of Frosted Flakes and milk
a small bag of M&Ms	a donut
a cup of hot cocoa	crackers and cheese
a big bowl of popcorn	a small bag of unsalted nuts
a peanut butter and jelly sandwich	a dish of ice cream

Writing ♣ *Describe your favorite meal. Write about when you eat it, how it tastes, how it is prepared, and why it is your favorite.*

The Noblest of Professions

full text on page 119 (cd track 7)

Introduction ❖

Every September teachers return to their classrooms ready to welcome a new group of students for the coming year. And every June they send their beloved students on to their next adventure. For a six-year-old, it means going into second grade. For a high school senior, it may mean college or a full-time job. And for college graduates who have majored in education, it means the beginning of the noblest of professions: teaching!

Vocabulary and Pronunciation ❖

1. **a guide** - a leader
2. **a counselor** - an advisor
3. **to measure** - to find the size, weight, speed, etc.
4. **a cheerleader** - a person who leads a crowd in support of a team
5. **self-esteem** - liking oneself, a sense of self-worth
6. **an optometrist** - an eye doctor who examines eyes and writes prescriptions for glasses
7. **a comedian** - a person who entertains others by using humor
8. **a psychiatrist** - a medical doctor who works with people who are having mental problems

Partial Dictation ❖

Here's what one writer has to say about teachers. Write the word or words you hear in the blank spaces. Discuss with a partner. Which ones do you like?

1. A teacher is a guide in the _____ ____ _____.

2. A teacher is a _____. The product is _____.

3. A teacher is a _____, a _____, and a healer of broken hearts.

4. A teacher is ____ _____ _____ than what a test can measure.

5. A teacher is a coach, a cheerleader, _____ ____ _____.

6. A teacher is a psychiatrist fostering _____ - _____ and an optometrist

   helping students _____ _____.

7. A teacher is an _____, a _____, and a storyteller.

8. A teacher is an X-ray technician _____ _____, a publisher at the copy

   machine, and a partner _____ _____ in the adventure of education.

Discussion ❖

Discuss the following items with a partner. Then share your ideas with the class.

1. What are some qualities of a good _____?
    a. teacher   b. student   c. accountant   d. parent

2. Rank these jobs according to how well-paid you think they are in the United States. Which jobs do not require a university degree?

    ___ airline pilot   ___ registered nurse   ___ electrician
    ___ mail carrier   ___ surgeon   ___ electrical engineer
    ___ criminal lawyer   ___ psychologist   ___ plumber

3. How happy are people with their jobs? Here are some comments that people make about their jobs. Which ones do you agree with and why?

    "I like working on a team."   "I like working alone."
    "I like to travel a lot."   "I'd go crazy sitting behind a desk all day."
    "I'm my own boss."   "There are lots of opportunities for advancement."
    "I get a good feeling of   "The hours are flexible."
     accomplishment."

4. Here are the ten most dangerous jobs in the U.S. according to the U.S. Bureau of Labor Statistics (2011). Can you guess which are the top five?

    ___ logging workers   ___ construction laborers
    ___ truck drivers   ___ natural resources workers/miners
    ___ farmers/ranchers   ___ fishermen
    ___ aircraft pilots/flight engineers   ___ trash and recyclable materials collectors
    ___ roofers   ___ structural iron and steel workers

Writing ❖

What are some qualities of a good teacher? Before you write your paragraph, read the following items and if you agree, include some or all of them in your composition. Explain why you chose the items.

A good teacher

- explains clearly
- knows the subject very well
- is strict
- cares about the students
- knows the answers to all of the students' questions
- prepares you for state tests
- is friendly, patient, and kind
- makes students figure out problems for themselves

Dear Mom and Dad

Introduction ❊

full text on page 120 (cd track 8)

Have you ever tried to prepare someone for bad news rather than telling them the bad news directly? This is what a college student tries to do in this letter to her parents.

Vocabulary and Pronunciation ❊

1. **thoughtless** - not caring, not considerate
2. **up to date** - to this point, so far, up to now
3. **I am getting along.** - I am doing well.
4. **a skull** - the bony framework of the head
5. **a fracture** - a break, particularly of a bone
6. **a concussion** - an injury to the brain caused by a hard blow
7. **a dormitory** - college housing
8. **open arms** - a warm, welcoming reception
9. **tolerance** - acceptance

Partial Dictation ❊

In the first part of the letter, fill in the blanks with the words you hear. In the second part of the letter put in the correct tense of the verb that is given . Correct and discuss the letter with a partner.

Dear Mom and Dad,

Since I left for college, I _____ _____ very bad about writing, and I am sorry for my thoughtlessness in not _____ written before. I will bring you up to date now, but before you read on, please sit down. You are not to read any further unless you are sitting down. OK?

Well then, I am getting along pretty well now. The skull fracture and the concussion I got when I _____ out of the window of my dormitory when it _____on fire is pretty well _____now. I only _____ two weeks in the hospital, and now I can see almost normally and only _____these sick headaches once a day. Fortunately, the fire in my dormitory and my jump _____ _____ by an attendant at the gas station near the dorm, and he was the one who _____ the fire department and the ambulance. He also _____me in the hospital, _____ ____ flowers, and since then we _____ _____ in love. We are _____ ____ marry, and I ____ _____ the university in order to find a job. He is _____ and has three young children that he _____ _____. This is difficult ____ ____ on a gas station attendant's salary, and I _____ _____.

Pairwork ✳ *The letter continues. With a partner, decide what form of the verb goes in each blank. The first two are done for you*

I __know__ (to know) that you __will welcome__ (to welcome) him into our family

with open arms. He _____ (to be) kind, and although not well educated he _____ (to be)

ambitious. Although he _____ (to be) of a different race and religion than ours, I know you

will not be _____ (to bother) by that.

Now that I _____ _____ (to bring) you up to date, I want to tell you that

there _____ (to be) no dormitory fire. I _____ _____ _____ (to not have) a concussion

or skull fracture. I _____ _____ (to not be) in the hospital and there _____ (to be) no

boyfriend in my life. However, I am _____ (to get) a D in history and F in science,

and I _____ (to want) you to see those marks in their proper perspective.

Your loving daughter,

Susan

Discussion ✳ *Discuss these questions with a partner. Share your answers and ideas with the class.*

1. Did the ending surprise you?
2. Do you think that Susan's parents put the "D" and the "F" in their proper perspective?
3. Can you think of an occasion when you prepared someone for the hard truth that you had to tell them?

Writing ✳ *Choose **one** of the following topics to write about.*

1. Write a letter to Susan from her mother and father in response to her letter.

2. There are many reasons for poor grades. List as many as you can, but a minimum of five.

   1. I didn't study for the test.

   2.

   3.

   4.

   5.

Thanksgiving

full text on page 121 (cd track 9)

Introduction ✤

Thanksgiving is a national holiday that is celebrated by all Americans. It is a time for families and friends to get together and give thanks for the good things in life. It was the first holiday celebrated by American colonists.

Before you begin, tell the class what you know about Thanksgiving.

Vocabulary and Pronunciation ✤

1. **a pumpkin** - a large, orange vegetable with a hard outside shell and soft insides with seeds
2. **tasty** - flavorful; yummy (slang)
3. **Pilgrims** - people who first came from Europe to the New World
4. **religious** - having strong beliefs in religion
5. **Indians** - people who are related to any of the original people of America; Native Americans
6. **to celebrate** - to do something special (like having a party) for a special event
7. **crowded** - full of people

Partial Dictation ✣

Listen and fill in the blanks. With a partner, decide if the statement is FACT or OPINION. A fact is a generally accepted statement of truth that you can check in a dictionary, encyclopedia, or other reference source. An opinion, on the other hand, expresses a personal feeling, idea, or point of view. Write F for Fact and O for Opinion. Share your answers with the class.

____1. Thanksgiving always comes on the _____ _____ in November.

____2. It is the _____ _____ American holiday.

____3. Many people have a big dinner that includes _____ and _____ _____.

____4. Turkey is tastier _____ _____.

____5. Thanksgiving dinners are ____ _____ ____ _____ to prepare.

____6. The Pilgrims started this tradition of _____ _____ in 1621.

____7. They came to Plymouth, Massachusetts, in 1620 to find_____ _____.

____8. They came ____ _____ _____ and didn't have enough food to eat.

____9. _____ _____ helped them by giving them food and showing them how ____

   _____.

___10. At the end of their first year in America, the Pilgrims _____ _____ Indians to

   celebrate with a _____ _____ in appreciation for their help in surviving their first year.

___11. Thanksgiving is _____ _____ travel holiday of the year. Airports are _____.

Discussion ✣ *Discuss another holiday with a partner. Include the following facts and opinions:*

1. The name of the holiday is _____.

2. It is a _____ holiday. (national, religious, children's)

3. We celebrate this holiday on _____. (date(s))

4. We have been celebrating this holiday for _____ years.

5. On this holiday, everyone _____, _____, and _____.
    (Talk about food, clothing, other customs)

6. This holiday is important because _____.

7. I like it because _____.

Writing ❖

Write a paragraph about a holiday or special day that is important to you. Use the points discussed above to guide you. Remember that there are different kinds of holidays or special events such as Mother's Day, Teacher's Day, and Children's Day.

We Shall Overcome

full text on page 122 (cd track 10)

Introduction ❖

The song "We Shall Overcome" became the song that Americans sang in their fight for racial equality. Singing helped give the civil rights protesters courage to go on. Listen to the song and sing along.

> We shall overcome
> We shall overcome
> We shall overcome some day.
> Deep in my heart
> I do believe
> We shall overcome some day.

Vocabulary and Pronunciation ❖

1. **1950's** - Read as "nineteen fifties"
2. **segregated** - separate; a segregated school can only be used by members of one race, religion, sex, etc.
3. **discrimination** - the practice of treating a person or a group differently from another in an unfair way
4. **a sit-in** - a peaceful non-violent method of protest
5. **facilities** - places or buildings used for a particular activity
6. **an ideal** - a principle or standard that you want to achieve

Partial Dictation ❖

Write the correct word in the blank space. With a partner, correct and discuss the dictation.

Although President Abraham Lincoln's Emancipation Proclamation set the slaves free during

_____ _____ _____ in 1865, blacks ____ _____ _____, especially in the South, still

suffered from unfair treatment because of _____ _____. Some states did not allow blacks

____ _____. Schools, buses, trains, and public businesses like theaters and restaurants were

segregated — separated into facilities for _____ _____ _____.

Imagine being a _____ _____, _____, or child in 1950 in Mississippi. You _____

_____ _____. You could go to school with black children only. You could drink only from a

separate water fountain, use separate bathrooms, swim in a separate swimming pool, and ride at

the _____ ___ _____ _____.

In the 40s and 50s, Presidents Roosevelt and Truman had said that discrimination based on race

and religion was against the ideals of _____ _____. However, it was not until 1954 that the Supreme Court said, "Separate educational facilities are inherently unequal." With this ruling, the Civil Rights Movement _____ _____. The courts ordered schools to be desegregated.

Now blacks had government support in their fight for equality, and the Civil Rights Movement _____ _____. It took ten years before the Civil Rights Act was passed by Congress. During that time many black citizens were holding peaceful marches and sit-ins ____ _____ ____ get voting rights and desegregated schools. They were often violently attacked by whites and even policemen armed with batons, bullwhips, fire hoses, _____ _____. But still they marched peacefully, singing "We Shall Overcome" while the world watched ____ _____.

The song "We Shall Overcome," _____ _____ a black gospel song, became the song of the _____ _____ Movement. It was sung during the sit-ins, voter registration drives, and protest marches of those heroic days. Since that time this song _____ _____ _____ by people _____ _____ the world who are fighting for equality or _____ _____.

Discussion ✤ *Discuss these questions with a partner. Share your ideas with the class.*

1. Do you know of any place in the world now where facilities are still segregated?
2. Do you know of any place in the world now where every citizen doesn't have equal rights?
3. Why does this happen?
4. Are there people in your country who had to fight for their right to vote?
5. Can anyone who comes to your country as an immigrant become a citizen?
6. Do you know any song(s) that people have sung in their fight for rights or freedom?
7. Do you think that racism has disappeared in the United States?

Writing ✤ *Write a paragraph (or more) about one of the seven discussion questions.*

Lacrosse

full text on page 123 (cd track 11)

Introduction ❋

The sport of lacrosse looks like a combination of basketball, soccer, and hockey. It is considered to be North America's first sport -- a game developed by many Native American nations, it was particularly popular among the First Nations of Canada. It is now one of the fastest-growing team sports in the United States.

With a partner, put this brief history of lacrosse in order from the earliest facts to the latest. The first one is done for you.

( ) Men's and women's lacrosse were played under the same rules until the mid-1930s.

(**1**) Lacrosse was first played centuries ago by North American Indians in preparation for war.

( ) Women's lacrosse in the U.S. was formed in 1926 at a school in Maryland.

( ) Lacrosse games evolved in Ontario, Canada, and in the U.S. in the 1600s.

( ) Those earliest games had as many as 1,000 players per side, from the same or different tribes.

( ) Lacrosse is currently a national sport with more than 250,000 active players.

( ) French-Canadian dentist George Beers standardized the game in 1867 with a new set of rules.

Vocabulary and Pronunciation ❋

1. **to scoop** - to pick up the ball with the lacrosse stick's net.
2. **agile** - quick and skillful in movement
3. **a financial reward** - money earned for doing something
4. **violent** - dangerous

Partial Dictation ✳

After you have filled in the blanks, work with a partner and decide if the statements are fact or opinion. Write F for fact or O for opinion on the line before each number. Discuss your answers.

____ 1. Lacrosse is played _____ ___ _____, the crosse, and the players need to

know how to _____, _____, and scoop.

____ 2. Lacrosse is a fast-paced sport and _____ ___ _____.

____ 3. _____ _____ _____ _____ than men because they are more agile.

____ 4. Most lacrosse players play for _____ ___ ____ _____ rather than for financial reward.

____ 5. Women's lacrosse is the best sport ____ _____ _____.

____ 6. Lacrosse is ___ _____ _____.

____ 7. Professional lacrosse in the U.S. has different rules and ____ _____ _____.

Discussion ✳ *With a partner, discuss these questions. Share your answers with the class.*

1. What sports do people play in other countries?
   What is the most popular sport in those countries?

2. Women are participating much more in school sports in North America.
   Is this happening elsewhere?

3. Who are some famous athletes from your country? Do they make a lot of money?

Cooperative Learning ✳

Work in four groups of three to five students. Using an encyclopedia or the Internet, each student finds out about one or more sports listed below and reports back to their group. Then all four groups present what they have learned.

Group 1	*Group 2*	*Group 3*	*Group 4*
1. croquet	1. rugby	1. rounders	1. petanque
2. paragliding	2. curling	2. futsal	2. hoop takraw
3. goalball	3. skydiving	3. disc golf	3. ultimate frisbee
4. haggi hurling	4. kabbadi	4. muay Thai	4. wiffleball
5. skeet shooting	5. endurance riding	5. hang gliding	5. fencing

Writing ✳

Option 1:

Choose one of these famous North Americans with some Native American Indian ancestry. Write a paragraph about them.

1. Jesse Jackson	4. Rita Coolidge
2. Johnny Depp	5. Angelina Jolie
3. Buffy Sainte Marie	6. Jimi Hendrix

Option 2:

Choose another sport that you know about and write a fact/opinion dictation similar to the one on the previous page.

Buying a Used Car

full text on page 124 (cd track 12)

Introduction ❄

Most people who buy a car, new or used, do not pay cash. They go to a bank and take out a car loan. Who you are, your job history, and credit record are all important. Here are two permanent residents who want to buy a used car. After you have the necessary information about these people, decide if they can afford to buy one.

Vocabulary and Pronunciation ❄

1. **a hybrid** - a gasoline-electric car
2. **a down payment** - a partial payment at the time of buying something
3. **a credit record** - a history of how you spend your money and pay your bills
4. **a loan** - money that you borrow
5. **an interest rate** - a percentage paid on an amount of money you borrow
6. **car insurance** - an agreement with a company in which the company will pay for a loss or accident
7. **a scholarship** - a loan or a grant that pays for education

Partial Dictation ❄

Listen and write the information about each person. Then work with a partner, check your notes with each other, and decide who can afford to buy a car.

Ashvin, age 19

How long in U.S.	_____	Price of used car	_____
How long driving	_____	20% down payment	_____
Present salary	_____/wk	% of interest	_____
Credit record	_____	Monthly payment	_____
Parents co-sign	_____	Car insurance	_____/ mo.

Shu Min, age 24

How long in U.S.	_____	Price of used car	_____
How long driving	_____	20% down payment	_____
Present salary	_____/yr	% of interest	_____
Monthly payment	_____	Credit record	_____
Car insurance	_____		

(Should she pay cash? _____ Why or why not?)

Discussion ❁ *Discuss these situations with a partner and decide what to do. Share your ideas with the class.*

1. Karl is looking at two used cars that he can afford. Which one should he buy? Why?

   Ford Fusion (2 years old)   **Ford Fusion, Hybrid (2 years old)**

       Price: $14,000   Price: $23,000

       Mileage: 25,000   Mileage: 14,000

       One-year warranty   Two-year warranty

       Miles per gallon: 22 city/33 hwy   Miles per gallon: 47 city/44 hwy

2. Rita, mother of three, can afford a new van. Which one should she buy? Why?

   Honda Odyssey (3 years old)   Toyota Sienna (2 years old)

       Price: $21,000   Price: $ 25,000

       Mileage: 20,000   Mileage: 15,000

       Miles per gallon: 19 city/28 hwy   Miles per gallon: 18 city/24 hwy

       Safety record: Excellent   Safety record: Excellent

Discussion ❋ *Discuss these items with a partner. Then share your ideas with the class. Your teacher will give you the answers.*

   1. Guess the names of the top five car companies, domestic and foreign, that Americans prefer.

      _____ _____ _____ _____ _____

   2. Of the top five, which do you think would be the top three in sales and in quality?

      _____ _____ _____

   3. Guess the car and model that has been the best seller in the U.S. for several years.

      _____

   4. What car features are important when you buy a car, new or used?

      miles per gallon   automatic/standard shift   color
      style   speed   air conditioning   comfort

   5. Last year, the prices of a Toyota Camry and a Honda Accord were approximately the same. If you shop around from dealer to dealer, you can often save $1000 or more.

   6. How do people usually buy a car – from a dealer, from classified ads, or from friends? Explain.

   7. Look at the used car ads in the automotive section of your local newspaper. Decide on a car that you might like to buy. Bring the ad to class and discuss it with a partner. Decide what questions you would ask the seller.

Writing ❋ *Write a paragraph about your "dream" car, truck, or motorcycle.*

Bullies

Introduction ❋

full text on page 125 (cd track 13)

Bullying is a big problem. It can make kids feel hurt, scared, sick, lonely, embarrassed, and sad. Bullies might hit, kick, or push to hurt people, or use words to call names, threaten, tease, or scare them. A bully might say mean things about someone, grab a kid's stuff, make fun of them, or leave a kid out of a group on purpose. Cyber bullying is also on the rise. Before you begin the dictation, talk about a bully you know or have heard of.

Vocabulary and Pronunciation ❋
1. **to pick on** - to bother or hurt someone; to tease
2. **to make fun of** - to tease or ridicule
3. **to shove** - to push hard with the hands
4. **a rumor** - information that comes from what other people say and may not be true
5. **to beat up** - to hit again and again and hurt
6. **to embarrass** - to cause someone to feel ashamed or self-conscious

Partial Dictation ❋

Listen and fill in the blanks. Then decide if you think the statement is true (T) or false (F). Write T or F on the line next to the statement. Discuss your answers with a partner and then with the class.

___ 1. Some bullies are _____ _____ _____.

___ 2. Most bullies _____ _____ or care about the _____ _____ others.

___ 3. Bullies often _____ _____ someone they think they have _____ _____.

___ 4. Most bullies are _____ _____ _____.

___ 5. _____ can make a school a place _____ _____ and can lead to _____ _____.

___ 6. Kids who are bullies cannot learn to _____ _____ _____.

___ 7. _____ _____ _____ _____ _____, it's important to tell an adult you can trust.

Discussion ❊

Talk about these situations with a partner. Discuss ways the bully should be handled.

1. Robert, 15, got into a fight in school with another boy named Charles. Charles, who started the fight, was often teasing and shoving Robert in the hallways. During the fight, Charles pulled off Robert's gold chain and kept it. He refused to return it. Robert is afraid to complain to his teacher because he doesn't speak English well.

2. Three girls – Jennifer, Laura, and Maria, all 15 – like the same boy, Paul. Paul called Maria and asked her to go to the movies. She said yes. Jennifer and Laura were jealous. They started saying bad things about Maria on line that aren't true. The rumors spread, and Maria is upset with their harmful lies.

3. Luis lived in fear of Brian. Everyday Luis would give his lunch money to Brian, but Brian still beat him up. He said that if Luis ever told anyone he would beat him up in front of all the other kids in class. Luis even cried one day and one of the girls told everyone that he was a baby and had been crying. Luis was embarrassd and felt really bad about himself and about school.

Discussion   ✳ *With the class, discuss the following statements.*

1. Parents should let children fight their own battles.
2. Most bullies come from unhappy families.
3. Children who are bullied will have problems later in life.
4. Teachers should call parents and tell them that their child is bullying other students.
5. Bullies are born, not made.

Writing   ✳ *Choose **one** of the two items below.*

1. Choose one of the statements in the discussion section above and write a paragraph about your opinion.

2. Write about an experience that you had that involved bullying (about a situation when you were bullied or when you bullied someone else).

The First Americans

full text on page 126 (cd track 14)

Introduction ❖

The earliest group of people to settle in North America are sometimes called American Indians or Native Americans. They had been living in North and South America long before any Europeans arrived. They were, indeed, the first Americans. Here is a brief history of their conflicts with European settlers.

Vocabulary and Pronunciation ❖

1. **an archeologist** - a person who studies human life and civilizations
2. **scattered** - gone in all directions
3. **to settle** - to move to an area and make a home
4. **harmony** - peaceful cooperation
5. **ownership** - belonging to a person or group
6. **to cheat** - to do something dishonest for gain
7. **unwillingness** - refusal to accept an action
8. **a reservation** - a land area set aside for native people to live on
9. **a battle** - a fight between enemy soldiers; a struggle
10. **a conflict** - a disagreement
11. **to end up** - to come to an end; to reach a conclusion
12. **mainstream** - the most popular way of thinking

Partial Dictation ❖ *Listen and fill in the blanks. Correct and discuss with a partner.*

Archeologists believe Native Americans (Indians) _____ _____ Asia 25,000 years ago. By the year 5,000 B.C., many different groups lived ____ _____ _____ of North America. Because Indians _____ ____ scattered groups and had little contact _____ _____ _____, they developed different cultures. They spoke _____ _____ different languages, wore different types of clothing, built different types _____ _____, and made their living _____ _____ _____. Those who settled in the northern areas _____ _____ _____. Those who settled in the east and southwest _____. Despite their many differences, _____ _____ shared the belief that people should live in harmony _____ _____. They believed that people should not own land because the land, like the air, stars, and water, _____ ____ _____. The European settlers _____ _____ the ownership of private property. These two very different _____ _____ _____ were the basis of the many conflicts between the Indians and the settlers.

In the early years of discovery and exploration between _____ and the mid-_____, relations with the Indians were, for the most part, _____. But as more and more settlers arrived, conflicts developed. Indian tribal leaders _____ _____ and angry because settlers were crowding people _____ _____ _____. When Indians "sold" land to the settlers, the Indians _____ _____ _____ they were only giving whites the right _____ _____ _____ _____.

Many settlers tried to understand the Indian way of life and treat them _____. But others _____ _____ and took their land. While Indians always fought _____ _____ _____, they were unable to stop the advance of thousands of settlers supported by the _____ _____. Indians won some battles, but they always ended up _____ _____ _____.

By 1880, fighting _____ _____. Finally, the government moved almost all the remaining Indians onto _____. Today, however, less _____ _____ of the Indians live on reservations. Those who do try to preserve their tribal _____ and ways of life. But discrimination by non-Indians, an unwillingness by Indians to _____ _____ _____, and a basic _____ _____ the federal government have kept many Indians out of the mainstream of _____ _____.

Navaho children

Discussion ❖ *Refer to the dictation in order to answer these questions with a partner.*

1. Why are there so many different Native American languages and cultures?
2. What was the basic difference in beliefs about land between the settlers and the Indians?
3. Why were Native Americans pushed farther west and eventually onto reservations?
4. Where are most Native Americans living today?
5. Many casinos are now on Indian reservation land, owned by the Indians and not regulated by the federal government. What is your opinion about this?

Writing and discussion ❖

Look up one of the following Indian tribes on the Internet. Write a summary of the article (or five interesting facts you learned) and tell the class about it.

Tribes: Hopi, Cree, Navaho, Iroquois, Mohawk, Apache, Wampanoag, Oneida, Comanche, and Arapaho. (If you want to, include one that is not listed here.)

Save Our Planet Award

full text on page 127 (cd track 15)

Introduction ❖

Do you think it is important to do something about pollution? Of course you do! We want our children to grow up in a healthy environment. Read and check (✔) the items you or your family can do to help save our planet. Talk about these items with the class.

(   ) take the bus or subway to save gasoline and lower air pollution
(   ) carpool to work or school to reduce traffic
(   ) take shorter showers to save water
(   ) turn down or turn off the air conditioner when you are not in the room to save electricity
(   ) recycle newspapers, bottles, and cans to save paper, glass, and metal
(   ) use low-energy light bulbs to save electricity
(   ) buy an electric-powered (or semi-electric) car to save on gasoline

Vocabulary and Pronunciation ❖

1. **recycling** - re-using waste products in a modified form, e.g. garbage to compost
2. **to volunteer** - to offer to do something without pay
3. **a reservoir** - a pond or lake that is used for drinking water
4. **a carpool** - a group of people who share a car and expenses by going places together
5. **plastic** - a strong, lightweight material made in a chemical process from oil or coal
6. **trash** - garbage; waste material
7. **a dump** - a place where you put trash   (dumping - dropping carelessly)
8. **to decompose** - to rot; decay

Partial Dictation and Discussion ❖

There are millions of people who want to save the environment! Some of them spend a lot of extra time volunteering to clean up the ocean, beaches, land, and roads. Every year, the Mayor of Greenland City, Mary Travis, gives a "Save the Planet" award to a group of people or an individual who helped keep their beautiful city clean and safe. You and your classmates will recommend a winner to Mayor Travis. Here are the three finalists.

Note: The city, the award, and the finalists are fictitious.

Fill in the blank spaces with the word or words you hear. Then discuss each candidate for the award with a partner. After you have chosen your winner, share your decision with the class. Then discuss all the decisions and vote for one winner.

A child recycling cans

1. **The Teen Team**.

   This _____ ____ _____ from Greenland Middle School saw a TV show

   about how plastic trash on beaches and ____ _____ _____ kills a million sea birds

   and fish every year. They organized a group of 15 student volunteers to _____

   _____, plastic bags, and plastic containers from their city's beaches every month.

   This has _____ _____ _____ of many birds and fish.

2. **Erin Brockton**.

   Erin and her children discovered that ___ _____ _____ in Greenland had

   been dumping poisonous chemicals in an _____ _____ near her neighborhood.

   Some of the poison had leaked into the reservoir where the town gets its _____

   _____. Many people got sick. After months ___ _____, Erin forced

   the paper company to find other, safer ways ____ _____ _____ ___ the waste.

3. **VFR (Volunteers for Recycling)**.

   These people spend a lot of time at _____ _____ _____. Why? Because they

   want to help Greenland residents _____ _____ _____,

   bottles, and cans. They also organized a "swap shop" at the dump where people could

   leave _____ _____ _____ _____, TVs, computers, and other _____

   _____. Then, people who need them can get them free. Their work has saved

   the town _____ ___ _____.

Discussion ❖ *With a partner, discuss these items. Share your ideas with the class.*

1. You want your friend to consider buying a hybrid car. This is a car that runs on electricity and gasoline. Your friend is not crazy about the idea because the car is a little more expensive than the other cars. What arguments can you use to help convince them?

2. Your sister has a new baby and is using disposable diapers. These diapers use up 1,265,000 metric tons of wood pulp and 65,000 metric tons of plastic that can take up to 500 years to decompose in a city dump. Can you convince your sister to use cloth diapers?

3. The orangutan, a large ape, is now an endangered species. There are many other animals in the world that are endangered. Can you name any? What can governments do to stop animal extinction?

Reading ❖ *You can make a difference!*

- If we recycle our Sunday papers, we can save over 500,000 trees every week.

- If every commuter car carried just one more passenger, we would save 600,000 gallons of gasoline and keep 12 million pounds of "greenhouse gases" out of the air every day.

- If we all installed "low-flow" shower heads, we could save billions of gallons of water every year.

Discussion ❖ *With a partner talk about the following:*

1. Do you have any environmental problems in your country or in the city where you are living now?

2. What are people doing in your city about environmental problems?

3. Do you care about any endangered animals? Which ones, and why?

4. How do you feel when you see or hear about environmental problems?

Writing ❖ *Write about A or B, below.*

A. Choose **one** of the questions in the preceding discussion and write a paragraph about it.

B. Write a paragraph explaining whom you chose as the finalist for the Save the Planet Award and why.

Privacy

full text on page 128 (cd track 16)

Introduction ❉

Privacy has disappeared. If you really want to know a lot about someone, you can google their name and immediately find out their age, telephone number, address, and many other things that used to be private.

Vocabulary and Pronunciation ❉

1. **blood pressure** - the force with which blood travels through your body
2. **How come?** - Why?
3. **I give up.** - "You win; I won't argue anymore."
4. **immediately** - at once
5. **overweight** - too heavy, fat
6. **privacy** - a condition of being able to keep your own affairs to yourself
7. **BLT** - a bacon, lettuce, and tomato sandwich

Partial Dictation ❉

Fill in the blank spaces with the words you hear. With a partner, correct and discuss the dialogue.

Operator: Thank you for calling Pizza Castle.

Customer: Hello, can I order...........

Operator: Can I have your multi-purpose _____ _____ first, sir?

Customer: Hold on . . . 123-12-_____.

Operator: Okay. _____ Mr. Saxe and _____ _____ from 26 Rose Lane. Your home number is 627-734-_____. Your office is _____-373-5716 and your cell _____ is 627-266-_____. Would you like to have this delivery made to 26 Rose Lane?

Customer: How _____ _____ _____ all my phone numbers?

Operator: We are connected to the system, sir.

Customer: _____ ____ _____ your Seafood Pizza?

Operator: That's not ____ _____ _____, sir.

Customer: How come?

Operator: According to _____ _____ _____ , you have high blood pressure and you're overweight.

Customer: This is crazy! _____ _____ _____ Seafood Pizzas.

Operator: That should be enough for _____ _____ _____ _____.

The _____ ____ $49.99, sir, and would you please pay _____ _____?

We see that _____ _____ _____ is over the limit.

Customer: I give up. You know everything _____ _____.

Discussion ❋ *Work with a partner and answer these questions.*

1. After you've corrected and discussed this dictation, read it aloud, with your partner taking one part and you taking the other part.
2. How much information do you think can be found out about you? Does this bother you?
3. What has made this possible? Is there anything we can do about it?

Listening ❋ *Listen to the dialogue and circle the correct answer.*

1. What is the waitress's name?
   a. Rina   b. Lily   c. Laura   d. Millie

2. What did the man order?
   a. a hamburger   b. a grilled cheese, bacon, and tomato sandwich
   c. a BLT   d. a grilled cheese and tomato sandwich

3. What kind of cheese did the man want?
   a. American   b. Swiss   c. cheddar   d. Havarti

4. What kind of bread did he want?
   a. wheat   b. rye   c. white   d. pumpernickel

5. What did he want to drink?
   a. espresso   b. tea   c. cappuccino   d. American coffee

6. What was he going to do while he waited?
   a. call someone on his phone   b. read the *New York Times*
   c. play a game on his iPhone   d. watch the other people in the restaurant

Writing ❋

Write a paragraph about the man in this dialogue. Describe everything you know about him.

What am I? An American?

full text on page 129 (cd track 17)

Introduction ✛

Amy Tan, author of several best-selling books including *The Joy Luck Club,* was born in California in 1952 to parents who immigrated from China in 1945 to escape the Chinese Civil War. Amy's novels center around the cultural norms and conflicts of Chinese-American families. At age 35, Amy first visited China with her elderly mother. The trip changed her life. In an interview, she was asked what advice she had for children of bicultural parents or first-generation children whose parents were born in another country.

Vocabulary and Pronunciation ✛

1. **a teenager** - someone aged 13 to 19
2. **ethnic identity** - a person's idea of their own heritage (cultural, linguistic, racial)
3. **first generation** - parents who came as immigrants
4. **poverty** - the state of not having much money; being poor

Partial Dictation ✛

Write the words you hear in the blank spaces. Correct and discuss the dictation with a partner.

For those of you first-generation children whose parents _____ _____

_____ _____ _____, let me tell you that, if you are confused, you

are not alone! When I was a teenager, I thought I was the only one _____ _____

_____. I asked myself, "_____ _____ _____? ____

_____?" Young people who have read my book, *The Joy Luck Club*, tell me,

"_____ _____ _____ _____ you've written my life. . . .

I'm the only kid in _____ _____- _____ _____

in all-white American schools. ____ _____ _____ _____

if I'm Chinese or not. What should I be?" When Amy was 35, she _____ _____

_____ _____ _____ _____ to the country of her parents. She

found out, _____ _____ _____ _____ _____; she found

out how American she was. _____ _____ _____!

Discussion ✛

Here are two more examples of Americans responding to questions about their identities.
Read them and compare their experiences to Amy Tan's.

1. Manny came to the U.S. from the Dominican Republic at age four as an illegal immigrant. He lived in homeless shelters in New York City with his mother and worked hard in school to learn English. He quickly realized that a good education was a ticket out of poverty. In high school he realized he couldn't have gotten the quality education at "home" that he got in the U.S. Manny says, "There are many things that I know about life in the Dominican Republic, but what I really know and love is here, in New York. I feel as American as anyone who was born here."

2. Kimberly, now 24, grew up in Florida with an American mother and a Palestinian father. Her father immigrated with his large family from Ramallah, a city six miles north of Jerusalem, when he was seven years old. People who know of Kimberly's father often assume she is Muslim. Her family is Christian, but she identifies herself as an Arab-American. While Kimberly is comfortable with being seen as an Arab-American, she knows that it can be difficult to find a place in American culture. She says, "Sometimes you feel like everyone in the world thinks if you're Palestinian, you're a terrorist."

Writing ✛

Ms. Tan says that it took her a long time to learn how to write the stories that ended up being
The Joy Luck Club. *She says, "At first, I wanted to write stories for myself and become good at it. Writing was very private. But those first stories were not from my own experiences. I made up things that were completely alien to my life. It took me a while to realize that you need to write about the things you know from your own experiences."*

Amy Tan

Option 1. Write about a person who has influenced you in your life. This might be a parent or other family member, a friend, or a teacher. Explain how this person helped you in some way.

Option 2. Write a short biography of a parent or friend who was born in another country.

❀ PAIR DICTATIONS ❀

Made . . . Where?

full text on page 130 (cd track 18)

Introduction ❀

Can you guess what percent of Americans own foreign cars? Can you guess which foreign car company sells the most cars in the U.S.? Do you know why some Americans refuse to buy a foreign car?

Vocabulary and Pronunciation ❀

1. **perking** - (short for percolating) - a liquid passing through a filter
2. **discouraging** - leading to a loss of hope or confidence
3. **fruitless** - useless; without benefit or results
4. **sandals** - simple footwear, usually with straps
5. **to pour** - to let flow; to release a liquid from a container
6. **to wonder** - to have an interest in knowing

Dictation ❋

For this dictation, work in pairs and dictate to each other. Student A (page 51) has half of the paragraph and reads their lines to Student B, who has the other half (A dictates and B writes). Then Student B (page 52) dictates and A writes until the paragraph is complete. When you are finished, check your paragraph with your partner.

❋ Student A ❋

Bill Smith started _____ _____ _____. He set his alarm clock (_____ ___ _____) for six o'clock a.m. While his coffeepot (_____ ___ _____) was perking, he shaved with his _____ _____ (_____ ___ _____ _____). He put on a dress shirt (_____ ___ _____ _____), designer jeans (_____ ___ _____), _____ _____ _____ (made in Korea).

After he cooked _____ _____ ___ ____ _____ _____ _____ (made in India), he sat down with his calculator (_____ ___ _____) to see how much ___ _____ _____ _____.

After he set his watch (made in Taiwan) ___ _____ _____ (made in India), ___ _____ ___ _____ _____ (made in Germany) and _____ _____ _____ for a good-paying American job. ___ _____ _____ ___ _____ _____ discouraging and fruitless day, Bill _____ ___ _____ for a while. He put on his sandals (_____ ___ _____), poured himself a _____ ___ _____ (made in France), and _____ ___ _____ ___ (_____ ___ _____), and then wondered why ___ _____ _____ ___ _____-_____ _____ in America!

Dictation ❀

For this dictation, work in pairs and dictate to each other. Student A (page 51) has half of the paragraph and reads their lines to Student B, who has the other half (A dictates and B writes). Then Student B (page 52) dictates and A writes until the paragraph is complete. When you are finished, check your paragraph with your partner.

❀ **Student B** ❀

_____ _____ _____ the day early. ____ _____ _____ _____

_____ (made in Japan) ____ ___ __ _____ ___ ___ . _____ ____

_____ (made in China) _____ _____, ___ _____ _____ ____

electric razor (made in Hong Kong). ___ _____ ___ _____ _____ _____ (made in

Sri Lanka), _____ _____ (made in Singapore), and tennis shoes (_____

___ _____).

_____ ___ _____ his breakfast in his new elecric fryer (_____ ___

_____), ___ _____ _____ _____ _____ _____ (made in Mexico) ____

_____ _____ _____ he could spend today.

_____ ___ _____ _____ _____ (_____ ___ _____) to the

radio (_____ ___ _____), he got in his car (_____ ___ _____) ____

continued his search _____ ___ _____ - _____ _____ _____ . At the

end of yet another _____ ____ _____ _____, _____ decided

to relax _____ ___ _____. ___ _____ ___ ____ _____ (made in Brazil),

_____ _____ ___ glass of wine (_____ ___ _____), _____ turned on

the TV (made in Indonesia), _____ _____ _____ _____ he couldn't find a good-

paying job ____ _____!

Discussion ✳ *Discuss these questions with a partner. Share your ideas with the class.*

1. From the dictation you can see that the U.S. imports products from all over the world. How does this affect the job market in the U.S.? Why are some products produced in other countries when it is possible to make them in the U.S.? Do you know what the minimum wage is in the U.S.?

2. What countries export these products? If you aren't sure, guess! You can name more than one country.

coffee _____	tea _____	shoes _____	oil _____
airplanes _____	cars _____	potatoes _____	beer _____
beef _____	rice _____	diamonds _____	wine _____
clothes _____	oranges _____	bananas _____	gold _____

Idioms and Expressions ✳ *Talk about the meanings of these expressions.*

She has a lot of get up and go.
Clothes make the man.
He always has a beef about something.
If the shoe fits, wear it.
He went bananas when he heard the news that she is now the top banana in the company.
She has a heart of gold, and she's worth her weight in gold.
The students burned the midnight oil before the exam.
The topic of the death penalty is a hot potato for politicians.

Writing ✳

Tourism is a major industry in many countries, especially those with tropical climates. Talk, then write about a place in the world you would like to visit, and explain why. Here are some possibilities:

Hawaii, London, Paris, Tokyo, Bali, Fiji Islands,
Rome, Puerto Rico, Montreal, Istanbul, Beijing,
Taipei, Dubai, Singapore, Mexico, Rio de Janeiro

How Honest Are You?

full text on page 131 (cd track 19)

Introduction ✳

If you lose a $100 bill on the street in most major cities in the world, would you expect someone to return it to a police station or a lost and found department?

Vocabulary and Pronunciation ❀

1. **to claim -** prove that something is yours and have it returned to you
2. **a metropolitan area -** a city and suburbs
3. **to hand in -** to give something to somebody in authority
4. **from early on -** from when you are young

Pair Dictation   ✳ *In the dictation here and on the next page, work in pairs and dictate to each other. Student A has half of the dictation and reads their lines to Student B, who has the other half (A dictates and B writes). Then Student B dictates and A writes until the dictation is complete. When you are finished, check your completed dictation with your partner.*

✳ Student A ✳

_____ ____ an article in the *New York Times* ____ _____ ____, _____,

titled "Never Lost but Found Daily: Japanese Honesty," ____ _____ _____ a $100 bill ____

_____, there is a good chance _____ ____ _____ ____ _____, and you

could claim it.

____ _____, with eight million people ____ _____ _____ and thirty-three million

____ _____ _____ _____, a $100 bill _____ _____ _____

_____ _____ to the Tokyo Metropolitan Police _____ _____ _____ _____.

In 2002, _____ _____ _____ _____ to the Tokyo Center _____-

_____ _____ in cash. 72% of it was returned ____ _____ _____ once

they had persuaded the police ____ _____ _____. About _____ went to the finders

_____ ____ _____ claimed the money _____ _____ ____ _____.

Children are taught _____ _____ ____ to hand in anything they find ____

_____ _____ in their neighborhood.

____ _____ _____ _____ _____ _____ is umbrellas, _____ ___

_____. The item _____ ____ _____ _____ ____ _____ is the cell phone, 75%.

Do people in your city return things they find? ____ _____?

Pair Dictation   ✳ *In the dictation here and on page 54, work in pairs and dictate to each other. Student A has half of the dictation and reads their lines to Student B, who has the other half (A dictates and B writes). Then Student B dictates and A writes until the dictation is complete. When you are finished, check your completed dictation with your partner.*

✳ Student B ✳

According to ____ _____ ____ ____ _____ _____ _____ on January 8, 2004, _____ "_____ _____ _____ _____ _____: _____ _____," if you lost ____ _____ _____ in Tokyo, _____ ____ __ _____ _____ that it would be returned, _____ _____ _____ _____ ___.

In Tokyo, _____ ____ _____ _____ in the city _____ _____- _____ _____ in the metropolitan area, _____ _____ _____ would probably find its way ____ _____ _____ _____ _____ Lost and Found Center.

____ _____, people found and brought ____ _____ _____ _____ twenty-three million ____ _____. _____ ____ ____ _____ _____ to the owners _____ _____ _____ _____ _____ _____ it was theirs. _____ 19% _____ ____ _____ _____ after no one _____ _____ _____ for half a year.

_____ _____ _____ from early on ____ _____ ____ _____ _____ _____ to the police ____ _____ _____.

The most frequently lost item ____ _____, 360,000 in 2002. _____ _____ with the highest rate of return ____ _____ _____ _____, _____.

____ _____ _____ _____ _____ _____ _____ _____ _____? Do you ?

Discussion   ✳ *Work with a partner and discuss these questions.*

1. Have you ever found anything? What did you do with it? Have you ever lost anything? What happened?

2. Do you think that if you live in an honest society, you are a more honest person, and that if you live in a dishonest society, you will probably be more dishonest?

3. Are you more honest if a small store owner would be hurt than if a large company or the government would be hurt? For example, would you return $10 to a small store owner if he gave you too much change by mistake? Would you return it to a large store like WalMart?

Discussion ❋

Discuss the following three situations with your partner and tell what you would do in each situation.

1. You've just checked into a hotel room and discovered an expensive watch near the phone. Would you call the hotel management and tell them about the watch?

ATM

2. When withdrawing money from an ATM, you receive an extra $200.00. Your account, however, doesn't show this. Would you keep the money?

3. The government has given you a large tax refund by mistake. Do you tell them?

Writing ❋ *Sometimes it is better to lie than to tell the truth. Do you agree or disagree?*

What's So Funny?

full text on page 131 (cd track 20)

Introduction ❊

In many cases Americans laugh at exactly the same things people in other countries laugh at. Here are two American jokes which we hope you will find funny. If you don't understand the joke, you say "I don't get it." The final line of the joke which should make you laugh is called "the punch line."

Vocabulary and Pronunciation ❊

1. **a tenant** - a person who is renting a house or apartment
2. **a tuba** - a large brass musical instrument that you play by blowing into it and that makes very loud, low sounds
3. **to stomp** - to walk with heavy steps, to put your foot down very hard, especially if you're angry
4. **urgent** - very important and needing to be done immediately
5. **a warning** - something that tells you that something bad, annoying, or dangerous might happen
6. **to yell** - to shout or say something very loudly
7. **yikes** - a meaningless word said when something frightens or shocks you

Pair Dictation ❈

In the dictation on this page and the next, work in pairs and dictate to each other. Student A will have half of the jokes and will read their part to Student B, who has the other half. Student A dictates and student B writes; then student B dictates and student A writes until each joke is finished. With your partner, correct the dictation and decide which joke you think is funnier.

❈ Student A ❈

Joke 1:

"Those people upstairs _____ _____ _____," complained the tenant. "_____

_____ they stomped and banged on the floor until midnight." " _____ _____ _____

_____?" asked the landlord. "_____," _____ _____ _____. "Luckily, I was

playing _____ _____."

Joke 2:

As a senior citizen _____ _____ _____ _____ _____, his car

phone rang. _____, he heard his wife's voice _____ _____

_____. "Herman, I just heard on the news that _____ _____ _____ _____ _____

_____ _____ on Route 280. I know you _____ _____ _____ _____,

so please be careful!" " _____," _____ _____, "it's not just ONE car. _____

_____ _____ _____!"

Pair Dictation ❋

In the dictation on this page and page 58, work in pairs and dictate to each other. Student A will have half of the jokes and will read their part to Student B, who has the other half. Student A dictates and student B writes; then student B dictates and student A writes until each joke is finished. With your partner, correct the dictation and decide which joke you think is funnier.

❋ Student B ❋

Joke 1:

"_____ _____ _____ are very annoying," _____

_____ _____. "Last night _____ _____ _____ _____ ____ _____

_____ _____ _____." "Did they wake you?" _____ _____

_____. "No," replied the tenant. "_____, ___ _____ _____ my tuba."

Joke 2:

_____ ____ _____ _____ was driving down the highway, _____ _____

_____ _____. Answering, ____ _____ _____ _____ _____ urgently

warning him. "_____, ____ _____ _____ ____ _____ _____ _____ there's a

car going the wrong way ____ _____ _____. ____ _____ _____ usually take Route 280,

____ _____ ____ _____!" "Yikes," yelled Herman, _____ _____ _____ _____

_____. It's hundreds of them!"

Discussion ❋ *Discuss the following with a partner.*

    1. Do you understand the two jokes?
    2. Which joke do you prefer?

Writing ❋ *Find a funny joke. Turn it into a dictation. Make copies and read it to the class.*

Eat That Insect?

Introduction ♣

full text on page 132 (cd track 21)

David Gordon, a science writer and author of *Eat-A-Bug Cookbook*, says that many insects are not only good-tasting but also good for you. He tasted his first bug ten years ago at a Seattle Museum event where Chex party mix was served with oven-baked crickets. To learn more about entomophagy, or bug-eating, try the dictation!

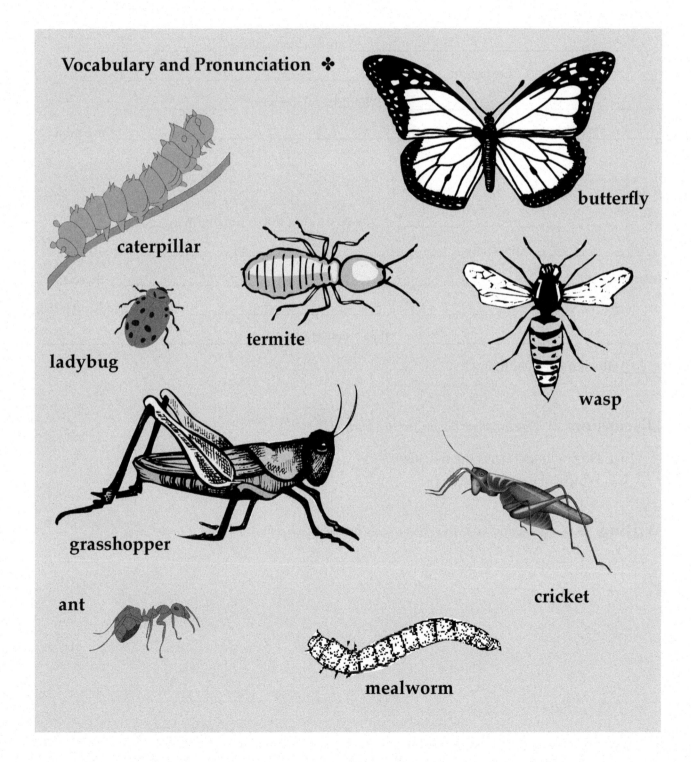

Vocabulary and Pronunciation ♣

caterpillar

butterfly

ladybug

termite

wasp

grasshopper

cricket

ant

mealworm

Pair Dictation ❖

In the dictation here and on the next page, work in pairs and dictate to each other. Student A will have half of the article and will read their lines to student B, who has the other half. Student A dictates and Student B writes, then Student B dictates and A writes until the passage is complete. Do not look at each other's pages!

❖ Student A ❖

Ladybugs are cute _____ _____ _____ _____, but most people who

come face to face _____ ____ _____ have one thought: _____ ____ ____! David

Gordon takes a different approach. ____ _____ _____ _____ _____ _____.

He thinks insects are a valuable, _____, _____ _____ _____

of nutrition. "If you're eating hot dogs, _____ _____ _____ _____ way

weirder than a grasshopper," said Gordon ____ ____ _____ _____ _____

_____ in an elementary school cafeteria. ____ _____ _____ ____ _____

grasshopper kebabs, fried crickets, and grilled mealworms. _____ _____

_____ _____ _____ from eating bugs, _____ _____

_____ _____ _____ _____ _____ _____ _____! But beware! Not all

bugs taste good, ____ _____ _____ _____, especially caterpillars. _____

_____ _____ _____ _____ do not want to eat them, which is why

_____ _____ _____ _____ _____ _____ thousands of trees each year.

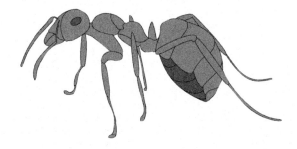

Pair Dictation ❖

In the dictation here and on page 61, work in pairs and dictate to each other. Student A will have half of the article and will read their lines to student B, who has the other half. Student A dictates and Student B writes, then Student B dictates and A writes until the passage is complete. Do not look at each other's pages!

❖ Student B ❖

_____ _____ _____ and butterflies are pretty, _____ _____ _____

_____ _____ _____ ____ _____ with an insect _____ _____ _____:

Step on it! _____ _____ _____ ___ _____ _____.

He cooks bugs and eats them. ____ _____ _____ _____ ____

_____, underused, and delicious source ____ _____. " ___

_____ _____ ____ _____, you're eating stuff that's _____ _____

_____ __ _____," _____ _____ as he demonstrated his cooking

skills ____ ___ _____ _____ _____. On his grill he

prepared _____ _____, _____ _____, _____

_____ _____. School rules prevented the children _____ _____

_____, but teachers tried them and thought they were tasty! _____ _____! _____

_____ _____ _____ _____, and some are poisonous, _____

_____. Even birds and other animals ___ _____ _____ ___ _____

_____, _____ ___ _____ some caterpillars can eat and destroy _____ ____

_____ _____ _____.

Discussion ❖ *Work with a partner and talk about these questions. Share your ideas with the class.*

1. How do you think the children in the school reacted when Gordon offered the cooked insects to the teachers?

2. Eating bugs is uncommon in the U.S., Europe, and Canada but routine in many other countries. For example, in Mexico people eat grasshoppers; in Indonesia people eat giant water bugs; in Africa they eat termites; in Japan they eat canned wasps; and in South Korea, they eat canned silkworm pupae. Have you tried any strange foods, such as frogs' legs, turtle soup, smoked dog, or chocolate ants?

3. Pretend that your boss invites you to dinner and serves grasshopper kebab. How would you react?

4. Is there one food that you just can't eat?

Insect Idioms and Expressions ❖ *Talk about the meanings of these sentences.*

1. He bugs me.
2. I told her to bug off.
3. I put a bug in his ear.
4. The phone was bugged.
5. He wormed his way into the conversation.
6. She has a bee in her bonnet.

Do you know that . . .

1. There are more kinds of beetles on earth than any other living creature.
2. Butterflies taste with their hind feet.
3. A cockroach can live several weeks with its head cut off.
4. An ant can lift 50 times its own weight.
5. Ants, ounce for ounce, contain twice as much protein as a sirloin steak.

Underage Drinking

full text on page 132 (cd track 22)

Introduction ✳

Here's a letter to an advice columnist about drinking and driving. Before you do the dictation, decide if the following statements are true or false. Discuss them with your classmates.

____ The legal drinking age in this state is 21.

____ The legal driving age in this state is 17.

____ The cost of car insurance is higher for people under 25 years of age.

____ In the U.S., motor vehicle accidents account for nearly 30% of all deaths among people aged 15 to 24.

Vocabulary and Pronunciation ✳

1. **can't afford** - not able to pay for
2. **to lend** - to allow someone to use something temporarily for a period of time
3. **fanatic** - extremely interested in something
4. **to persuade** - to lead someone to believe or do something

Dictation ✳

In this dictation, work in pairs and dictate to each other. Student A has half of the letter and reads to Student B, who has the other half. (A dictates and B writes.) Then Student B dictates and Student A writes until the letter is complete. When you finish, check your letter with your partner.

❖ Student A ❖

Dear _____,

   I am _____, and though I _____ _____ _____ _____

_____, I can't afford to buy my own car, _____ _____ _____

_____ my parents'. _____ _____ _____ about lending it

to me _____ _____ _____ fanatic on the subject _____

_____ _____ _____. I know that drinking

_____ _____ _____, but I also know _____

____ _____ _____ _____ after drinking only two beers.

_____ _____ _____ persuade my parents _____ _____

_____ _____ _____?

                              George from Georgetown

Dictation ✳

In this dictation, work in pairs and dictate to each other. Student A has half of the letter and reads to Student B, who has the other half. (A dictates and B writes.) Then Student B dictates and Student A writes until the letter is complete. When you finish, check your letter with your partner.

❖ Student B ❖

_____ Deena,

_____ _____ 17, _____ _____ _____ feel I am an adult, _____

_____ _____ _____ _____ _____ _____ _____, so I

must use _____ _____. They are good _____ _____

_____ _____ _____ but are absolutely _____ _____ _____

_____ of drinking and driving. _____ _____ _____

_____ causes many accidents, _____ _____ _____ _____ that I

can drive safely _____ _____ _____ _____ _____.

How can I _____ _____ _____ to see that it's OK?

George from Georgetown

Role plays ✳

The class should be organized in groups of 3 or 4. Each group will create one of the scenes below and act it out for the class. Students have 10 minutes to create and practice. No writing is necessary. Decide what role you are going to play and what you are going to say as the scene develops. Each person should assume a role and a point of view. If you prefer not to assume a point of view, just present the discussion and the class will suggest a solution. Be sure you understand the problem!

1. Scene one:
   George wants to drive his parents' car and thinks it's okay to drive after only drinking two beers.

2. Scene two:
   Mary, age 21, a student, was arrested for driving drunk and has to pay $4000 for a lawyer, court costs, fines, and an alcohol education program. She tries to persuade her parents to help with the costs.

Writing ✳ *Choose **one** of the following.*

1. Write a letter persuading a friend or parent to allow you to do something.

2. Write a paragraph responding to George.

I've Always Wanted to Be a Nurse

Introduction ❊

full text on page 133 (cd track 23)

How do people choose careers? Little children often want to be firefighters, police officers, astronauts, dancers, or actors. As they grow older, they usually choose professions that are less dangerous and more realistic. What did you want to be when you were a child? In this dictation Nora tells us why she's happy she's a nurse.

Vocabulary and Pronunciation ❊

1. **pediatrics** - medical care for children
2. **stressed** - feeling mental pressure
3. **surgery** - the treatment of injury or disease by cutting

Pair Dictation ❊

In this dictation, work in pairs and dictate to each other. Student A has half of the dictation and reads to Student B, who has the other half. (A dictates and B writes.) Then Student B dictates and Student A writes until the dictation is complete. When you finish, check the whole dictation with your partner.

❖ Student A ❖

I've wanted _____ _____ a nurse _____ _____ _____ a little girl. _____

_____ _____ _____ bandages _____ _____ _____.

I know that _____ _____ _____ _____,

_____ _____ _____ I feel like _____ _____ _____

_____. It's great _____ _____ someone get well.

However, it can be _____ _____ at times. _____

_____ _____ _____ _____ work nights, weekends,

and holidays.

_____ _____ _____ _____ _____ _____ _____

25 years. _____ _____ _____ in pediatrics and

surgery. _____ _____ _____ _____

_____ anything else.

Pair Dictation ✳

In this dictation, work in pairs and dictate to each other. Student A has half of the dictation and reads to Student B, who has the other half. (A dictates and B writes.) Then Student B dictates and Student A writes until the dictation is complete. When you finish, check the whole dictation with your partner.

♣ Student B ♣

_____ _____ to be _____ _____ since I was _____ _____

_____. I used to put _____ on my dolls. _____ _____

_____ nursing isn't for everyone, but every day _____ _____ _____

I'm making a difference. _____ _____ to see _____ _____

_____.

_____, _____ _____ _____ very stressful _____ _____.

Also I've often had to _____ _____, _____, _____ _____.

But I've been a nurse for _____ _____. I've loved working _____

_____ _____ _____. I can't see myself doing _____ _____.

Discussion ❋ *Discuss these questions with a partner. Share your ideas with the class.*

1. What does the writer say are the advantages and disadvantages of being a nurse? Can you think of any others that are not mentioned?

2. In recent years, more and more nurses are men. Can you think of any reasons for this?

3. Are you suited to nursing? Would you be a good nurse? Why?

4. The writer mentions pediatrics. Pediatrics is the medical specialty dealing with children, and the doctor is called a pediatrician. Here are five other specialties. Find out what they mean and then add three of your own to share with the class.

Specialty	Doctor	What is it?
1. obstetrics	obstetrician	
2. cardiology	cardiologist	
3. dermatology	dermatologist	
4.		
5.		

Writing ❀

Write about the advantages and disadvantages of a job you have now, or a job you've had in the past, or a job you'd like to have.

Cooperative Learning ❀

Work in four groups with the same number of students in each group. Below are four sets of occupations, and each group is assigned one of these sets. Each person in the group finds out what one or more of the people in these sets does and then reports back to their group. This can be done as homework or in class. Each person in the group must be prepared to explain all the occupations in their set. Then all the people are reassigned to newly configured groups. Finally each person shares with their new group what they have learned about the occupations.

Set 1

Receptionist
Umpire
Accountant
Dramatist
Bus boy
Crane operator

Set 3

Plumber
Head of State
Mason
Architect
Antiques dealer
Orthodontist

Set 2

Cab driver
Computer analyst
Sous chef
Social worker
Consul
Linguist

Set 4

Butcher
Headmistress
Massage therapist
Probation officer
Exterminator
Maitre d'

Kimchi

full text on page 134 (cd track 24)

Introduction ✤

In almost all cultures people believe that there are certain foods that you should eat to prevent certain illnesses and other foods that you should eat when you are sick so you will get well quickly. In the past in some countries, families sent their children to school in the winter with little bags of garlic tied around their necks to keep flu and colds away. In many countries, if you have a cold or the flu, some form of chicken soup is the answer to getting better quickly. For Koreans, kimchi is an essential food that will prevent you from getting sick. If you get sick, kimchi will help you get well.

Vocabulary and Pronunciation ✤

1. **cabbage** - a large round vegetable with thick green or purple leaves
2. **a chili pepper** - a small type of pepper with a very strong spicy taste
3. **fermented** - changed chemically, as when sugar is converted into alcohol
4. **garlic** - a plant like a small onion or radish with a very strong taste, used in cooking
5. **kimchi** - the Korean national dish
6. **over-the-counter drugs** - medicines, like aspirin, that you can buy without a prescription
7. **to stock up on** - to buy or gather goods to keep for a later time

Pair Dictation ✤

In this dictation, work in pairs and dictate to each other. Student A has half of the dictation and reads to Student B, who has the other half. (A dictates and B writes.) Then Student B dictates and Student A writes until the dictation is complete. When you finish, check the whole dictation with your partner.

✤ Student A ✤

It is just fermented cabbage, _____, _____ _____ _____, but

Asians buy _____ _____ of kimchi, _____ _____

_____ _____ is really _____ _____ _____.

Southeast Asians _____ _____ ___ ___ ___. It's _____ _____

in China. And South Koreans, _____ _____ ____ with every meal, _____ _____ _____

_____ _____, hoping its healing powers _____ _____ ____ _____.

"I can't imagine ___ _____ _____ ____," said a housewife. "_____

_____ _____ _____ _____ a lot of it. _____ _____ _____

that they are healthy _____ _____ _____ a lot of kimchi."

_____ _____ _____ says this theory may be _____

_____ _____, but that doesn't mean it doesn't work.

Making Kimchi

Pair Dictation ✤

In this dictation, work in pairs and dictate to each other. Student A has half of the dictation and reads to Student B, who has the other half. (A dictates and B writes.) Then Student B dictates and Student A writes until the dictation is complete. When you finish, check the whole dictation with your partner.

✤ Student B ✤

____ ___ _____ _____ _____, garlic, and chili peppers, _____ _____ _____ large amounts _____ _____, hoping Korea's national dish _____ _____ a wonder drug.

_____ _____ are stocking up on it. _____ very popular _____ _____. _____ _____ _____, who eat it _____ _____ _____, are buying more than usual, _____ _____ _____ _____ will make it famous.

"_____ _____ _____ a meal without it," _____ _____ _____. "I'm making my children eat _____ _____ _____ _____ . I certainly believe _____ _____ _____ _____ because they eat ____ _____ _____ _____."

A Korean scientist _____ _____ _____ _____ _____ difficult to prove, _____ _____ _____ _____ ____ _____ _____.

Discussion ❖ *With a partner, discuss the following questions.*

1. Folk medicine beliefs and practices differ from culture to culture. They are passed on from person to person by word of mouth and imitation. Most cures and remedies depend on what is close at hand to treat illnesses. They include things like soda, garlic, sugar, whiskey, vinegar, plants, mud, vodka, and mustard.   Here are some examples:
    - for hair loss, rub your head with half an onion before you go any balder.
    - for a sore throat, mash an onion into pulp and add a little water until you have onion juice, and gargle. (Needless to say, don't do this before a date.)

2. What remedies have you heard about from your parents or grandparents that are traditional, rather than something your doctor prescribes or that you buy over the counter at a pharmacy?

3. Have you ever tried one of these remedies?

Idioms ❖

Here are some common idioms or expressions. Can you and your partner guess what they mean?

1. Give someone a taste of their own medicine.
2. Laughter is the best medicine.
3. She's a real pill.
4. That's a bitter pill to swallow.

Writing ❖ *Choose **one** of the following topics.*

1. Why do people use folk remedies? List as many reasons as you can.
2. Make a list of folk medicine recipes that you and your classmates know about.

Subway Manners

full text on page 134 (cd track 25)

Introduction ❋

How do you get to school or work? Do you walk, bike, drive, or use public transportation? What do you like or dislike about public transportation? This dictation gives some suggestions for making everyone's time on the subway or bus more pleasant.

Vocabulary and Pronunciation ❋

1. **annoying** - making one feel slightly angry
2. **messy** - not neat
3. **one-sided** - hearing only one side of a conversation
4. **pregnant** - carrying an unborn baby
5. **to stare** - to look continuously
6. **disabilities** - problems with parts of the bodies – broken legs, blindness, deafness, etc.

Pair Dictation ❋

In this dictation, work in pairs and dictate to each other. Student A has half of the dictation and reads to Student B, who has the other half. (A dictates and B writes.) Then Student B dictates and Student A writes until the dictation is complete. When you finish, check the whole dictation with your partner.

♣ Student A ♣

1. Do you read _____ _____ on the train? _____ _____

   in your own space. _____ _____ with you _____ _____

   _____.

2. Turn your cell phone off. _____ _____ _____ to listen _____ _____

   _____-_____ conversation.

3. _____ _____ smelly, messy, _____ _____ _____ on a train or bus.

4. _____ _____ at other passengers.

5. _____ _____ _____ to people with disabilities, _____ _____,

   and pregnant women.

Pair Dictation ❋

In this dictation, work in pairs and dictate to each other. Student A has half of the dictation and reads to Student B, who has the other half. (A dictates and B writes.) Then Student B dictates and Student A writes until the dictation is complete. When you finish, check the whole dictation with your partner.

❖ Student B ❖

1. _____ _____ _____ a newspaper _____ _____ _____?

   Keep it _____ _____ ____ _____. Take it _____ _____

   when you leave.

2. _____ _____ _____ _____ ____. No one wants _____ _____

   to your one-sided _____.

3. Don't eat _____, _____, or sticky foods ____ ____ _____ ___ _____.

4. Don't stare _____ _____ _____.

5. Offer your seat _____ _____ _____ _____, elderly people, _____

   _____ _____.

Discussion ❋ *With a partner, discuss the following questions*

1. Can you think of other good rules to help people enjoy the subway more?

2. You are a young man and tired after a long day of work. A woman gets on the train and stands in front of you. Do you offer her your seat?

3. You are on a crowded train. Suddenly the cell phone in your backpack rings. It is your best friend calling. Do you begin a long, gossipy conversation?

4. You get on the train and you are starved. Do you take out a tuna fish sandwich from your lunch bag and begin to eat?

Writing ❋ *Choose **one** of the following topics.*

1. What is one of the best or worst experiences you've had on a bus, subway, or train?

2. Compare public transportation in a city you have lived in with transportation in the city you are now living in.

The Top Six and the Top Three

full text on page 135 (cd track 26)

Introduction ❀

Here's a fun activity, Guess the top three answers!

Vocabulary and Pronunciation ❀

1. **a lumberjack** - a person who cuts down trees
2. **adultery** - sex between a married person and another person who is not their spouse

Pair Dictation ✳

In this dictation, work in pairs and dictate to each other. Student A has half of the dictation and reads to Student B, who has the other half. (A dictates and B writes.) Then Student B dictates and Student A writes until the dictation is complete. When you finish, check the whole dictation with your partner, and then guess the top three. The answers are on page 135.

♣ Student A ♣

1. What are the six most common excuses ____ _____ _____ ____ _____ _____?

   a. My dog ate it.
   b. I left it on the bus.
   c. I was sick.

   d. I lost it.
   e. I spilled orange juice on it.
   f. There was a power failure.

2. Where can a single woman _____ ____ _____ ____?

   a. a bookstore
   b. online
   c. a museum

   d. a coffee shop
   e. a library
   f. a university

3. _____ ____ ____ _____ American desserts?

   a. cupcakes
   b. brownies
   c. chocolate chip cookies

   d. apple pie
   e. fruits and cheese
   f. ice cream

4. _____ ____ _____ American Sunday dinners?

   a. roast beef
   b. pasta
   c. hamburgers

   d. baked chicken
   e. fish/seafood
   f. pork roast

5. Name the reasons _____ _____ _____.

   a. money problems
   b. drug/alcohol use
   c. imprisonment

   d. differences that can't change
   e. adultery
   f. mental and physical abuse

6. _____ ____ _____ _____ most dangerous jobs?

   a. roofer
   b. pilot
   c. lumberjack

   d. iron and steel worker
   e. trash/recyclable collector
   f. fisherman

Pair Dictation ✳

In this dictation, work in pairs and dictate to each other. Student A has half of the dictation and reads to Student B, who has the other half. (A dictates and B writes.) Then Student B dictates and Student A writes until the dictation is complete. When you finish, check the whole dictation with your partner, and then guess the top three. The answers are on page 135.

♣ Student B ♣

1. _____ ____ ____ ____ _____ _____ _____ for not handing in your homework?

   a. My dog ate it.
   b. I left it on the bus.
   c. I was sick.

   d. I lost it.
   e. I spilled orange juice on it.
   f. There was a power failure.

2. _____ ____ ____ _____ _____ meet an intelligent man?

   a. a bookstore
   b. online
   c. a museum

   d. a coffee shop
   e. a library
   f. a university

3. What are the favorite _____ _____?

   a. cupcakes
   b. brownies
   c. chocolate chip cookies

   d. apple pie
   e. fruits and cheese
   f. ice cream

4. What are typical _____ _____ _____?

   a. roast beef
   b. pasta
   c. hamburgers

   d. baked chicken
   e. fish/seafood
   f. pork roast

5. _____ _____ _____ why Americans divorce.

   a. money problems
   b. drug/alcohol use
   c. imprisonment

   d. differences that can't change
   e. adultery
   f. mental and physical abuse

6. What are the three _____ _____ _____?

   a. roofer
   b. pilot
   c. lumberjack

   d. iron and steel worker
   e. trash/recyclable collector
   f. fisherman

Cooperative Learning Fun – What would Americans say? ❋

Work in four groups with the same number of students in each group. Below are four sets of occupations, and each group is assigned one of these sets. Each person in the group chooses answers to one or several of the questions in their group's set and then reports back to their group. This can be done as homework or in class. Each person in the group must be prepared to answer all the questions in their set. Then all the people are reassigned to newly configured groups. Finally each person shares with their new group what they have learned about the questions they have discussed. The answers are on page 136.

Set One

1. Name the best age to marry.
2. Name a sport played with a small ball.
3. Name two ways Americans can get rich quickly.
4. Name a very common American last name.
5. Name the three largest American states in size.

Set Two

1. Name four fruits that begin with the letter P.
2. Name a sport that looks easier than it is.
3. Name two organizations that help people in trouble.
4. Name a type of bird you hope you never eat.
5. Name a good food to warm you up on a cold night.

Set Three

1. Name something you own that was made in a foreign country.
2. Name a sport that is played in the water.
3. Name a state many Americans go to for vacation.
4. Name a word that rhymes with "shake."
5. Name the most famous writer of English/American literature of all time.

Set Four

1. What's the most you would pay for a movie ticket?
2. Name three U.S. states with large populations.
3. Name a young and famous singer and actor, female or male.
4. Name three foods a college student with little money might eat.
5. What's the first thing you do when you get up in the morning?

Opportunity Knocks

full text on page 137 (cd track 27)

Introduction ❖

A newly arrived immigrant had an opportunity, took it, and was successful.

Vocabulary ❖

1. **traumatized** - not able to do things normally because of a very bad experience
2. **a mentor** - an experienced person who advises, encourages, and helps a less experienced person
3. **to turn down** - to refuse
4. **to kidnap** - to catch and hold a person – usually for a ransom (money)
5. **a scholarship** - money given for education either for excellence or need

Prediction Dictation ❖

In this activity you are not going to listen first. Work with a partner and fill in each blank with a word you think is correct. When you are finished, you will listen and do the dictation on the next page. Then compare your responses.

Most _____ schools will not accept young people who are _____ 17, have a history of school troubles, speak little _____ , or otherwise seem unlikely to be able ____ _____ the final exams and graduate in a reasonable amount of _____.
____ New York, a night _____day school _____ created for these students.

Four_____ ago, just before his sixteenth _____, Jean-Luc Gerard landed at Kennedy _____with $20.00 in his _____, alone, speaking no _____, and traumatized by the deaths of his uncle and brother in a West African civil war. _____ mother _____ kidnapped, and he _____ saw her again.

Four _____ later Mr. Gerard _____ graduated from this high school with a full _____ to Dartmouth College. He had been a night student while _____full-time during the _____. The teachers helped _____ with tutoring. They _____ him English. They _____ him with immigration and gave him a mentor. The mentor even gave him a party when he was _____ to college.

More than half the students at the _____are recent _____ like Mr. Gerard. Most come to school during the day for intensive _____ classes after they have been turned down by other high schools because of their age. No one at the school has much _____. Many students at the school hold some kind of _____ to support _____, their children, and sometimes other family _____.

Listening Dictation ❖

Listen and fill in the blanks with the words you hear. Correct and discuss the dictation with your partner.

Most _____ schools will not accept young people who are _____ 17, have a history of school troubles, speak little _____, or otherwise seem unlikely to be able ____ _____ the final exams and graduate in a reasonable amount of _____. ____ New York, a night _____ day school _____ created for these students.

Four_____ ago, just before his sixteenth _____, Jean-Luc Gerard landed at Kennedy _____ with $20.00 in his _____, alone, speaking no _____, and traumatized by the deaths of his uncle and brother in a West African civil war. _____ mother _____ kidnapped, and he _____ saw her again.

Four _____ later Mr. Gerard _____ graduated from this high school with a full _____ to Dartmouth College. He had been a night student while _____ full-time during the _____. The teachers helped _____ with tutoring. They _____ him English. They _____ him with immigration and gave him a mentor. The mentor even gave him a party when he was _____ to college.

More than half the students at the _____ are recent _____ like Mr. Gerard. Most come to school during the day for intensive _____ classes after they have been turned down by other high schools because of their age. No one at the school has much _____. Many students at the school hold some kind of _____ to support _____, their children, and sometimes other family _____.

Discussion ❖

Work with a partner. Share your ideas with the class.

1. What kind of future will Mr. Gerard have after he graduates from college?
2. What are some of the difficulties that he had to overcome in order to graduate from high school and receive a scholarship?
3. If you are an immigrant, what difficulties did you have to overcome, and still have to overcome?
4. Has anyone helped you? Who? Did it make a difference?

Dartmouth College

Writing ❖ *Choose **one** of the following topics.*

1. Write a paragraph about an opportunity you have had since you arrived in this country.

2. Do you have a lot of contact with others who came from your native country? In what ways do you help each other out?

3. Have you found what you were looking for in this country? Please explain.

Overprotected?

full text on page 138 (cd track 28)

Introduction ❋

Parents love their children. No matter how old they are, they worry about them and try very hard to keep them away from danger. Some parents try too hard to protect their children. Were you overprotected when you were a child?

Vocabulary and Pronunciation ❋

1. **overprotective** - so anxious to protect someone from harm that you restrict their freedom
2. **foreigner** - someone from a different country
3. **to pressure** - attempt to persuade someone by using influence, argument, or threat
4. **commute** - to travel from home to school or work and back
5. **prom** - a formal dance party for high school students
6. **on your own** - alone, by yourself
7. **instinct** - a natural tendency to behave or react in a particular way without having to learn about it or think about it

Prediction Dictation ❋ *This is a letter to an advice columnist. Work with a partner and decide on a word to fill in each blank space.*

Dear Amy,

I read you _____ the Internet because I _____ in Europe. I am _____ to a foreigner and _____ in his country. I love it here, but my problem is the difference in attitude about children. Specifically, I _____ a nine-year-old daughter who must take a bus to the train _____ and then a 20-minute _____ on a train to get to her school. It is a private bilingual _____. Many of the _____ in her _____ come from far _____ on their _____. In fact, this is quite common in their culture. Children are off to school on their _____ as young _____ kindergarten. I am American and my instinct is not to allow a nine-year-old to go through a big city train _____ on _____ _____. My husband and my daughter's teacher have been pressuring me; she _____ I am overprotective, that I should let my daughter make this trip ____ _____. I am just _____ comfortable with this. Am I overprotective? How can I ever _____ comfortable about this?

Kate

Listening Dictation ✻ *Listen and fill in the blanks with the words you hear. Then compare your prediction to the listening with a partner.*

Dear Amy,

I read you _____ the Internet because I _____ in Europe. I am _____ to a foreigner and _____ in his country. I love it here, but my problem is the difference in attitude about children. Specifically, I _____ a nine-year-old daughter who must take a bus to the train _____ and then a 20-minute _____ on a train to get to her school. It is a private bilingual _____. Many of the _____ in her _____ come from far _____ on their _____. In fact, this is quite common in their culture. Children are off to school on their _____ as young _____ kindergarten. I am American and my instinct is not to allow a nine-year-old to go through a big city train _____ on _____ _____. My husband and my daughter's teacher have been pressuring me; she _____ I am overprotective, that I should let my daughter make this trip ___ _____. I am just _____ comfortable with this. Am I overprotective? How can I ever _____ comfortable about this?

Kate

Discussion ✳ *Discuss these questions with a partner. Share your ideas with the class.*

1. Do you believe that Kate is being overprotective?

2. What do you think the mother is afraid of?

3. Are you now living in a country where children have more freedom than they do in your original country?

Discussion ✳ *Discuss the following situations.*

A. Your nine-year-old daughter's friend is having a "sleep-over" birthday party. The party begins with dinner at 6:00 p.m. and you are told to pick up your child at 10:00 the following morning. Do you let your child go?

B. High school seniors stay out all night on the night of the senior prom. The night begins with a dinner dance at a hotel, followed by a party at someone's house, and ends with breakfast at a popular restaurant. Your daughter really wants to go but your husband disapproves. What do you do?

C. Your three-year-old wants to climb to the top of a very big slide and then go down it herself. She screams when you try to help her. Do you let her do it alone?

Writing ✳ *Choose one of the following topics and write several paragraphs.*

1. Write a response to Kate, giving her advice.
2. Write about the negative and/or positive effects of being overprotective.
3. Write about a time in your life when you were overprotective or a time when you were overprotected.

A Tour of Washington, D.C.

Introduction ✣

full text on page 139 (cd track 29)

Have you ever gone on a tour when you were on vacation? Here is a tour guide leading a group around Washington, D.C., the capital of the United States.

Vocabulary and Pronunciation ✣

1. **start off with a bang** - begin suddenly with something fun and exciting
2. **a hop, skip, and a jump** - nearby, a short distance

Prediction Dictation ✣

In this dictation you are not going to listen first. Work with a partner and fill in each blank with a word you think is correct. When you are finished, you will listen to the dictation on the next page. Then compare your responses.

Good morning, ladies and _____, boys and _____. My name is George, and I am your personal tour guide. For the _____ six hours, we _____ be exploring exciting Washington, D.C., the _____ of the United States. Let's start off with a bang and visit the _____ House, D.C.'s _____ popular tourist attraction. Who knows, _____we'll even get to _____ the President at work in the Oval Office. Then it's only a hop, skip, and a jump to the Smithsonian Institution, where you _____ probably spend a whole week; there's so much to _____. Then it's on to the Lincoln Memorial. If you ask a hundred Americans who the greatest _____ of the U.S. was, most will say Abraham Lincoln. That's because he signed the Emancipation Proclamation to free the slaves. And here's the Big One! For lunch, we're _____ to the Capitol Building Cafeteria, where you'll get to _____ famous politicians. You may even ask them to sign their autographs for the low, low, low price of $50. HA! HA! HA! All aboard!

Listening Dictation ❖ *Listen and fill in the blanks with the words you hear. Then compare your prediction to the listening with a partner.*

Good morning, ladies and _____, boys and _____. My name is George, and I am your personal tour guide. For the_____ six hours, we _____ be exploring exciting Washington, D.C., the _____ of the United States. Let's start off with a bang and visit the _____ House, D.C.'s _____ popular tourist attraction. Who knows, _____we'll even get to _____ the President at work in the Oval Office. Then it's only a hop, skip, and a jump to the Smithsonian Institution, where you _____ probably spend a whole week; there's so much to _____. Then it's on to the Lincoln Memorial. If you ask a hundred Americans who the greatest _____ of the U.S. was, most will say Abraham Lincoln. That's because he signed the Emancipation Proclamation to free the slaves. And here's the Big One! For lunch, we're _____ to the Capitol Building Cafeteria, where you'll get to _____ famous politicians. You may even ask them to sign their autographs for the low, low, low price of $50. HA! HA! HA! All aboard!

Discussion ❖ *With a partner, discuss the following items. Share your answers with the class.*

1. Have you ever been to Washington, D.C.? If so, tell the class about it.

2. Tell your group about the best (or worst) vacation you have ever had.

3. Make a list of the main tourist attractions in a city you know, or the city you are living in now. Tell your group why everyone should see these places.

4. You are visiting a famous place, like Hollywood, CA, and you have only three hours, so you decide to take a bus tour. What are some advantages and disadvantages of taking a bus tour?

Writing ❖

Arrange these sentences in chronological/logical order. Before you write, check your answers with a partner. Then write them in paragraph form.

_____ They planned to leave at 2:00 on Friday.

___1___ John wanted to go to Washington, D.C.

_____ They promised to study hard.

_____ And he couldn't afford to fly.

_____ He begged her to drive to D.C.

_____ On Thursday John's advisor told him to study harder.

_____ Unfortunately, he doesn't know how to drive.

_____ She refused to drive to D.C.

_____ So they decided not to go to D.C.

_____ She finally agreed to drive to D.C.

_____ Mary's professor also advised her to study.

_____ So he asked Mary to drive to D.C.

Writing ❖ *After discussing your best (or worst) vacation, write a paragraph about it.*

International Women's Day

full text on page 140 (cd track 30)

Introduction ✛

Every year on March 8th, people all over the world celebrate International Women's Day. It is a day to honor women's accomplishments in the areas of politics, economics, art, and the humanities. One winner in 2012 was Hana El Hebshi from Libya. In the photograph she is standing between Michelle Obama and Hillary Clinton. She was honored for her work as an architect.

Vocabulary and Pronunciation ✛

1. **an accomplishment** - an achievement, a successful effort
2. **humanities** - areas of study (art, music, literature, philosophy, etc.)
3. **to honor** - praise, give recognition
4. **domestic violence** - physical attacks (usually on women) in the home

Prediction Dictation ✛

In this dictation you are not going to listen first. Work with a partner and fill in each blank with a word you think is correct. When you are finished, you will listen to the dictation on the next page. Then compare your responses.

International Women's Day _____ a day to honor _____ praise women for their accomplishments. In some _____, such as China, Russia, and Zambia, _____ is an official holiday. In _____ countries, such as _____ United States, it is not a _____ holiday, but people celebrate _____. Some _____, such as Mother Teresa from Calcutta, India, have received _____ for their work with the poor. Others, such as Aung San Suu Kyi of Myanmar and Wangari Maathai _____ Kenya, _____ honored for their work to make their _____ government serve its _____ better. Over the years _____ progress has been made in _____ parts of the world, but women still have a long _____ to go.

Listening Dictation ❖

Listen and fill in the blanks with the words you hear. Then compare your prediction to the listening with a partner.

International Women's Day _____ a day to honor _____ praise women for their accomplishments. In some _____, such as China, Russia, and Zambia, _____ is an official holiday. In _____ countries, such as the United States, it is not a _____ holiday, but people celebrate _____. Some _____, such as Mother Teresa from Calcutta, India, have received _____ for their work with the poor. Others, such as Aung San Suu Kyi of Myanmar and Wangari Maathai _____ Kenya, _____ honored for their work to make their _____ government serve its _____ better. Over the years _____ progress has been made in _____ parts of the world, but women still have a long _____ to go.

Discussion ❖ *Work with a partner and answer these questions.*

1. Name a famous woman from your country. Why is she important?
2. Who is Michelle Obama? Hillary Clinton? Explain some of their accomplishments.
3. Why is it important to honor women?
4. What countries need to pay more attention to women and women's rights?
5. Below is a list of issues that women are working on in many countries. Tell what you know about:

    domestic violence

    the right to vote

    the closing of public schools to women

    equal pay for equal work
6. Check the accomplishments of women you know about. Can you name one?

    _____ astronauts   _____ prime ministers   _____ university professors

    _____ athletes   _____ company presidents   _____ architects

Writing ❖ *Choose one of the following.*

1. Write about a famous woman from your country and her accomplishments.
2. Write about an issue in your country that women are still working for.

Too Much Clutter

full text on page 140 (cd track 31)

Introduction ❖

Can a marriage be happy when people have different lifestyles? What should Carol do?

Vocabulary and Pronunciation ❖

1. **can't stand** - strongly dislike
2. **clutter** - a lot of unnecessary things occupying space
3. **guilty** - the feeling that you have when you know you have done something wrong
4. **a lifestyle** - the way you live
5. **on the other hand** - showing contrast
6. **a pack rat** - a person who keeps collecting things and never throws them away
7. **to reread** - to read again

Prediction Dictation ❖

In this dictation you are not going to listen first. Work with a partner and fill in each blank with a word you think is correct. When you are finished, you will listen to the dictation on the next page. Then compare your responses.

Dear Dora,

     My husband and I _____ been married for thirty-two _____ . It _____ a good marriage. We are _____ happy, _____ there is one problem.

Alan _____ a pack rat. He never throws anything _____. For example, he _____ two newspapers _____ day and he keeps them around the _____ in case he wants to reread an article. Most of the time _____ never does. He also keeps things like broken watches and old clothes that he _____ in high _____.

     On the other hand, I usually throw _____ things I will never use again. Sometimes when my husband is out of the _____, I throw away some ____ his things, and I don't tell him about _____. I feel a little guilty, but I can't stand so much clutter. What should I do?

                                    Carol

Listening Dictation ❖

Listen and fill in the blanks with the words you hear. Then compare your prediction to the listening with a partner.

Dear Dora,

My husband and I _____ been married for thirty-two _____ . It _____ a good marriage. We are _____ happy, _____ there is one problem. Alan _____ a pack rat. He never throws anything _____ . For example, he _____ two newspapers _____ day and he keeps them around the _____ in case he wants to reread an article. Most of the time _____ never does. He also keeps things like broken watches and old clothes that he _____ in high _____ .

On the other hand, I usually throw _____ things I will never use again. Sometimes when my husband is out of the _____ , I throw away some _____ his things, and I don't tell him about _____ . I feel a little guilty, but I can't stand so much clutter. What should I do?

Carol

Discussion ❖ *Discuss these questions with a partner..*

1. Do you usually throw out things that you know you will never use again or do you keep them? Why?
2. Do you sympathize with Carol or do you think she is doing something wrong?

Writing ❖

Write a letter from Dora to Carol giving her advice about what to do.

What's the Best Way to Discipline Kids?

Introduction ❖

full text on page 141 (cd track 32)

Parents in sixteen countries were asked how they discipline their children. The respondents came from Asia, Europe, North America, South America, and Australia. Can you guess which items were the best approaches to use in all countries?

Vocabulary and Pronunciation ❖

1. **to discipline** - to teach someone (especially children) to behave well
2. **to misbehave** - to act badly, to be impolite
3. **physical punishment** - rough body contact; a slap; a spanking
4. **a privilege** - a special right or benefit given to a person
5. **scolding** - speaking angrily to someone telling them what they did was wrong

Prediction Dictation ❖

In this dictation you are not going to listen first. Work with a partner and fill in each blank with a word you think is correct. When you are finished, you will listen to the dictation on the next page.

1. **Talk about It!**

   "To teach _____ children _____ lesson, I prefer _____ talk to them about what _____ did wrong. My two _____ often misbehave, but they always react better to a conversation than a scolding." (***Mexico***)

2. **Take Away a Privilege**

   "I prefer to take away _____ children's computer and texting privileges when they _____ to be disciplined. I do this _____ talking doesn't work." (***U.S.***)

3. **Send Them to Their Rooms**

   "You have to discipline _____ kids. But pain can't teach _____ as much as love can. I send them to _____ rooms." (***China***)

4. **Physical Punishment**

   "Sometimes a spanking _____ necessary. I think it works _____ children ages 5 to 8." (***Russia***)

Listening Dictation ❖

Listen and write what you hear in the blank spaces. Which form of discipline do you think is the best? Decide if you agree or disagree with the statements. Write A for Agree or D for Disagree on the line next to the statement. Women's answers may vary from men's.

____ 1. **Talk about It!**

"To teach _____ children _____ lesson, I prefer _____ talk to them about what _____ did wrong. My two _____ often misbehave, but they always react better to a conversation than a scolding." (***Mexico***)

____ 2. **Take Away a Privilege**

"I prefer to take away _____ children's computer and texting privileges when they _____ to be disciplined. I do this _____ talking doesn't work." (***U.S.***)

____ 3. **Send Them to Their Rooms**

"You have to discipline _____ kids. But pain can't teach _____ as much as love can. I send them to _____ rooms." (***China***)

____ 4. **Physical Punishment**

"Sometimes a spanking _____ necessary. I think it works _____ children ages 5 to 8." (***Russia***)

Discussion ❖ *Work with a partner and talk about your decisions.*

1. Do you agree or disagree with the four statements? Give reasons why.
2. Do you think that people in your country would agree with you? Would your parents?
3. Do you think that men have different ideas about discipline than women?
4. Do you think countries should have laws about disciplining kids?

Writing ❖

1. Parents should never hit their children. Do you agree or disagree?
2. Some people think you should send children who misbehave to their rooms. What are some of the advantages and disadvantages of this?

Toys for Girls, Toys for Boys

Introduction ❖

full text on page 141 (cd track 33)

Do only little girls play with dolls? Are toy trucks mostly for boys? Do you think that toys should be gender neutral or do you think there are real differences between what little boys and little girls prefer?

Vocabulary and Pronunciation ❖

1. **a female** - a woman, a girl
2. **a male** - a man, a boy
3. **gender neutral** - something that applies to both females and males
4. **a manufacturer** - a company that makes things
5. **a petition** - a request in writing for somebody to make a change
6. **an oven** - the part of a stove that you bake or roast food in
7. **upset** - worried or unhappy

Prediction Dictation ❖

In this dictation you are not going to listen first. Work by yourself or with a partner and fill in each blank with a word you think is correct. When you are finished, you will listen to the dictation on the next page. Then compare your responses.

Recently a thirteen-_____-old girl wanted _____ give _____ four-year-old brother a gift for Christmas. She wanted to _____ him an "Easy-Bake Oven" because he likes to help _____ mother bake cookies.

There _____ a problem. She looked at the ads. All of the _____ were pink or purple, and all of the ads showed little _____ with the toy ovens.

The girl, McKenna Pope, was upset. Why were toy ovens only for _____? She got 40,000 _____ to sign a petition and sent it to the manufacturer, Hasbro, a big toy company. She was successful. Now there _____ also "Easy-Bake Ovens" in blue, silver, and black, and the ads have _____ playing with the _____, as well.

Listening Dictation ✛

Listen and fill in the blanks with the words you hear. Then, with a partner, compare your prediction with the listening.

Recently a thirteen- _____-old girl wanted _____ give _____ four-year-old brother a gift for Christmas. She wanted to _____ him an "Easy-Bake Oven" because he likes to help _____ mother bake cookies.

There _____ a problem. She looked at the ads. All of the _____ were pink or purple, and all of the ads showed little _____ with the toy ovens.

The girl, McKenna Pope, was upset. Why were toy ovens only for _____? She got 40,000 _____ to sign a petition and sent it to the manufacturer, Hasbro, a big toy company. She was successful. Now there _____ also "Easy-Bake Ovens" in blue, silver, and black, and the ads have _____ playing with the _____, as well.

Discussion ✛ *With a partner, discuss the following exercise.*

Do you think that some toys are more for boys or for girls? Beside each toy put F for female (girls), M for male (boys), or B for both. Then discuss each with your partner.

_____ soccer ball　　　　_____ jump rope　　　　_____ paper dolls

_____ jigsaw puzzle　　　_____ doll　　　　　　_____ building blocks

_____ toy gun　　　　　_____ roller skates　　　_____ stuffed animal

_____ Frisbee　　　　　_____ board game (chess, Monopoly, etc.)

_____ skateboard　　　_____ coloring book and crayons

Writing ✛

Write about a favorite toy you had as a child. How old were you? Who gave it to you? How did you play with it? Describe it.

Pampered Pooches

Introduction ❖

full text on page 142 (cd track 34)

Even when times are difficult and many people don't have jobs, pet boutiques continue to do well. There are always people who spend a lot of money on extravagant gifts for their dogs. They say that it is important for them to pamper their beloved pet because their dog is the most important thing in their life.

Vocabulary and Pronunciation ❖

1. **a pooch** - a positive slang word for a dog
2. **beloved** - dearly loved
3. **billions** - one billion = 1,000,000,000
4. **cashmere** - soft, expensive wool
5. **a collar** - something worn around the neck
6. **extravagant** - spending or costing a lot of money
7. **to pamper** - to treat a person or pet very well

Prediction Dictation ❖

In this dictation you are not going to listen first. Work by yourself or with a partner and fill in each blank with a word you think is correct. When you are finished, listen to and do the dictation on the next page. Then compare your answers.

What do _____ buy for a person who has everything? That _____ a common question. A new question _____, what do you _____ for a dog who _____ everything?

Pet spending is _____ over 50 billion _____ per year, up from 45 billion _____ a few _____ ago. Dogs wear Ralph Lauren cashmere _____, Burberry raincoats, and diamond collars, and have boxes _____ toys.

93% of dog _____ consider their _____ to be members of _____ family. They enjoy _____ things for their _____.

Listening Dictation ✛

Listen and fill in the blanks with the words you hear. Then, with a partner, compare your prediction with the listening.

What do _____ buy for a person who has everything? That _____ a common

question. A new question _____, what do you _____ for a dog who _____ everything?

Pet spending is _____ over 50 billion _____ per year, up from 45 billion

_____ a few _____ ago. Dogs wear Ralph Lauren cashmere _____, Burberry

raincoats, and diamond collars, and have boxes _____ toys.

93% of dog _____ consider their _____ to be members of _____

family. They enjoy _____ things for their _____.

Listening ✛

There are eight good reasons listed below for owning a dog. Listen to the recording, and when you hear one of these reasons, put a ✔ beside it.

_____ 1. You will feel safer if there is a dog in the house.

_____ 2. You will relax more and reduce everyday stress.

_____ 3. You will increase your physical activity because you will have to walk your dog.

_____ 4. A dog will help reduce your heart rate and lower your blood pressure.

_____ 5. A dog can help you adjust to serious illness or death; you can turn to it for comfort.

_____ 6. Families feel happer if they have a dog.

_____ 7. Dogs give elderly people who live alone a reason for living.

_____ 8. A dog makes us feel less lonely.

Discussion ✛ *Work with a partner and talk about your decisions.*

1. Do you own a dog? Have you ever owned a dog?
2. Do many people in your country own dogs? What is a popular breed of dog in your country?
3. Do you or have you ever owned a different kind of pet?

Writing ✛

Write about a pet you own, have owned, or would like to own. Or write about why you wouldn't want to own a pet.

Little People of America

Introduction ❖

full text on page 143 (cd track 35)

Little People of America can be children or adults. They can be young or old. They are people who are born with a condition called dwarfism. It affects about 50,000 people in the United States. Adults with dwarfism are 4-foot-10 or smaller. A national organization called Little People of America, Inc. is a 5000-member non-profit group that provides support for people who are short. Here is an interview with Amy Watson, age 23, who is three feet tall. She is attending a worldwide conference on dwarfism in Massachusetts.

Vocabulary and Pronunciaton ❖

1. **stature** - how tall you are; your height
2. **gene** - the basic part of a living cell that contains characteristics of one's parents
3. **conception** - the beginning moment of life
4. **pregnancy** - the condition of a mother having a baby developing in her uterus
5. **a disability** - a disadvantage or handicap
6. **the spinal cord** - the thick nerve that runs through the bones (spine) in the back
7. **orthopedic** - a part of medicine that specializes in problems in the bones
8. **a workshop** - a small group of people who work together on a project or idea
9. **neurology** - the study of the nervous system and its disorders
10. **the guy scene** - where available men can be found

Dictogloss Pre-Listening ❖

Listen to each sentence only once and write down the words you can remember. With a partner, try to reconstruct the sentences in writing as accurately as possible. Before doing the listening below, talk about/guess the possible answers to the three questions in this pre-listening activity.

1. _____

2. _____

3. _____

Listening ❖

    You will listen to an interview between a reporter and a woman, Amy, with achondroplasia, a form of dwarfism. Amy is at a conference for people with her condition. First, just listen and check (✓) the sentences you hear on the CD. Then work with a partner to check your answers.

_____ 1. What are the causes of dwarfism?

_____ 2. It's a chemical change within a single gene that begins during conception.

_____ 3. Most dwarfs suffer from ill health.

_____ 4. Nine out of ten children born with this condition have average-sized parents.

_____ 5. Achondroplasia is a rare form of dwarfism.

_____ 6. Some of us have spinal and orthopedic problems.

_____ 7. People here instantly connect, and it's like "wow!"

_____ 8. I met someone, and I'm in a long-term relationship.

_____ 9. There are workshops for families and friends.

_____ 10. I'm definitely going to check out the guy scene!

Discussion ❖ *Talk about these issues with a partner.*

1. A person with achondroplasia has one dwarfism gene and one "average size" gene. If both parents have achondroplasia, there is a 25% chance their child will be average size. There's a 50% chance the child will be a dwarf. And there is a 25% chance the child will die at birth or shortly afterwards. What advice do you think a doctor would give to an achondroplasic couple who want to have a family?

2. Scientists say that genetic screening for achondroplasia in fetuses is available (along with tests for other genetic defects). Do you think that this condition will become extinct in the future?

3. One term that is not acceptable in the LP (little people) community is "midget." This is an old term that used to be associated with carnival shows and circus acts. In other words, "midgets" were seen as freaks. There are other offensive words for other minority groups such as Italians, African-Americans, and Asians. Share words that you know, and discuss why these words are disrespectful.

4. At the conference there are workshops touching on parental concerns such as safety issues, teasing, self-esteem, and the raising of teenagers with dwarfism. What specific types of questions do you think these parents and relatives would have for social workers and psychologists?

5. Little people often disagree over whether they are part of the disabled community. Those who say "Yes, we are disabled" are working together to get the government to make new regulations with short people in mind. This is because LPs have problems at services such as ATMs and gas pumps, and would like to see their needs accommodated like those of the handicapped. What other problems do you think LPs would run into?

Writing ❖

You are the parent of a 10-year-old child in a wheelchair.
List the extra responsibilities that you would have.

Homeschooling

full text on page 145 (cd track 36)

Introduction ❖

Homeschooling, the education of children at home by their parents or guardians, has gained in acceptance in the past 35 years. A recent estimate of the number of children in the United States who are schooled at home is approximately two million. The following is an interview with a parent who homeschooled her daughter, Eve, for five years. Eve is now enrolled in Michigan State University.

Vocabulary and Pronunciation - (meanings limited to this context only) ❖

1. **to/a challenge** - to test one's abilities; something that's difficult but not impossible
2. **conservative Christians** - people who want to include more (Christian) religion in their children's education
3. **an approach** - a course of action
4. **a virtual course** - a computer course that is taken only online
5. **expertise** - a special skill in doing something
6. **to network** - to meet and exchange information with people in similar situations
7. **isolated** - separated from others

Dictogloss Pre-Listening ❖

Listen to each sentence only once and write down the words you can remember. With a partner try to reconstruct the sentences in writing as accurately as possible. Before doing the listening below, talk about/guess the possible answers to the three questions in this pre-listening activity.

1. _____

2. _____

3. _____

Listening ✛

You will listen to an interview with a parent who homeschooled her daughter. Listen twice. The first time, just listen. The second time, listen and check (✓) the sentences you hear. Then work with a partner to check your answers.

_____　1.　We didn't want to send her to private school.

_____　2.　At home she will be excited about learning and be challenged.

_____　3.　Two million children are now homeschooled.

_____　4.　In the 1980's and 90's, it became more popular.

_____　5.　We can buy lesson plans in all subjects from organizations and schools.

_____　6.　We parents share our expertise and have support groups.

_____　7.　All parents of homeschooled children have college degrees.

_____　8.　I do most of the teaching during the day.

_____　9.　We have this network of activities that put homeschoolers together.

_____　10.　Eve has many friends in her neighborhood.

Discussion ❖ *With a partner, talk about these statements.*

A.　Decide if these statements are Fact or Opinion.

(　) 1.　Private schools are more expensive than public schools.

(　) 2.　Private schools are better than public schools.

(　) 3.　Homeschooling is now legal in all 50 states.

(　) 4.　Homeschooling is better than the public schools.

(　) 5.　Homeschooling started back in the 1970's.

B.　Decide if these statements are True or False -- or write IDK (I don't know)

(　) 1.　Eve and her parents are very religious.

(　) 2.　Eve was bored in public school.

(　) 3.　Eve's parents both graduated from four-year universities.

(　) 4.　Eve's mother does most of the teaching.

(　) 5.　Eve received excellent grades in her courses.

(　) 6.　Eve has opportunities to socialize with others her age.

(　) 7.　You can't get accepted into a university if you have been schooled at home.

(　) 8.　Homeschooled students are better prepared to enter a university than other students.

C. Talk about these questions with a partner. Share your ideas with the class.

1. According to Eve's mother, what are some advantages of homeschooling?

2. What concerns do you have about homeschooling?

3. What other questions would you have for Eve's parents?

4. More African-American and Latino parents are homeschooling their children. Here are some of their complaints about public (and parochial) schools. Which do you agree/disagree with?

> overcrowded classrooms
>
> underqualified teachers
>
> bullying by racists
>
> too much emphasis on passing tests

Idioms ❖ *Discuss the meaning of these idioms and expressions with your class*

1. She's conservative. She's from the old school.
2. He's a socialist. He belongs to that school of thought.
3. He was schooled in the family business.
4. She's learning the ropes on her new job.
5. Sandra is the teacher's pet.
6. Bob's a smart aleck – a "know-it-all."
7. She knows her p's and q's.
8. She has the know-how to do her job well.

Writing ❖

From your notes, write a summary of the interview. You may take each question individually and respond in complete sentences or write a paragraph highlighting the important information.

What's in a Name?

Introduction ❋

full text on page 147 (cd track 37)

"What's in a name?" wrote Shakespeare. "A rose by any other name would smell as sweet." Nevertheless, we give great importance to names. In some cultures the baby receives the name of a favorite relative who has died. In other cultures, the first- born male child receives the same name as his father with one small difference. In an English-speaking culture, if the father is Wilson Smith, Sr. (Senior), the baby becomes Wilson Smith, Jr. (Junior). When Wilson Smith, Jr., has a baby, that baby may be called Wilson Smith, III (the third).

Vocabulary and Pronunciation ❋

1. **male** - man, masculine
2. **nowadays** - at the present time

Partial Dictation ❋

Write the correct words in the blank spaces. With a partner, correct and discuss the dictation.

Some people name their children after _____ _____ or famous people. In the 1940's many girls _____ Shirley _____ _____ after a child actress, Shirley Temple. Nowadays we _____ _____ children named Celine and Brad.

When people from other _____ come to the United States, _____ as international students or as _____, they often change their names and _____ English names. They do this _____ _____ reasons. First, English speakers may have _____ understanding and _____ their names correctly. Second, people may have _____ _____ their names. Third, because they are in a new country, they may want _____ _____ their lives and begin with a new name.

Dictogloss ❖

Listen to each sentence only once and write down the words you can remember. With a partner, try to reconstruct the entire sentence and write it below. Then talk about your responses.

1. _____

2. _____

3. _____

4. _____

5. _____

Discussion ❖   *Discuss these questions with a partner. Share your ideas with the class.*

1. Do you know the meaning of your name? What is it?

2. Have your parents ever told you why they gave you your first name?

3. Have you ever taken a new name? Why and how did you choose it?

4. Are you upset when someone does not pronounce your name correctly? Do you correct them?

Writing ❖

Choose one of the topics above or one of the following two to write about.

1. When a baby is given a name, there is often a religious or cultural ceremony performed at the same time. If this is done in your country or culture, describe and discuss it.

2. When people marry in the United States, there may be a change of names. For example, when Barbara McDonald marries Richard Cogan, she can choose to become Barbara Cogan-McDonald, Barbara McDonald Cogan, or Barbara Cogan, or she can remain Barbara McDonald. Richard Cogan can choose to remain Richard Cogan, or he can change his name to Richard Cogan-McDonald or Richard McDonald Cogan. Describe how names change in your culture when people get married.

Driver's Licenses for Illegal Immigrants?

Introduction ✳

full text on page 148 (cd track 38)

According to the Immigration and Naturalization Service, legal immigration to the U,S, varies between 700,000 and 900,000 people each year. The agency also estimates that 420,000 illegal aliens enter the country every year. The total number of illegal aliens is about 7,000,000, most of whom are from Mexico. There is a lot of discussion about the rights and privileges of illegal immigrants.

Vocabulary and Pronunciation ✳

1. **a privilege** - a benefit or special right given to a person
2. **a criminal** - a person who commits a serious crime
3. **car insurance** - an agreement with an insurance company in which the company will pay for damage or liability in exchange for regular payments
4. **medical coverage** - medical insurance
5. **allowed** - permitted
6. **alien** - belonging to another country

Dictogloss Dictation ✛

Listen to each sentence only once and write down the words you can remember. With a partner, try to reconstruct the entire sentence and write it below as accurately as possible.

The following five people were asked, "Should illegal immigrants be allowed to obtain driver's licenses?" Here are their responses. When you are finished, discuss the opinions with a partner.

1. Karen Johnson

_____

2. Jason Garcia

_____

3. Helen Chen

_____

4. David Peterson

_____

5. Minnie Lee

_____

Fact or Opinion? ✳

With a partner, decide if the statement is a FACT or OPINION. A fact is a generally accepted true statement, whereas an opinion expresses a personal feeling or point of view. Write O for opinion and F for fact. Share your answers with the class.

( ) 1. There are too many immigrants in the United States.

( ) 2. 75% of illegal immigrants come from Mexico.

( ) 3. The U.S. government is not doing enough to help immigrants.

( ) 4. The U.S. government shouldn't try to help illegal immigrants.

( ) 5. The U.S. government deports only 1% of illegal aliens.

Discussion ✳ *With a partner, talk about these issues.*

1. Several years ago, Walmart, a large company that now has 4,700 stores in the U.S., got into trouble for hiring illegal immigrants to clean their stores at night. If a company knows it is hiring illegal immigrants, it may be taken to court and face criminal and civil penalties. How can companies know if a person is legal or not?

2. Nine of the 250 illegal immigrants who were arrested have decided to sue Walmart. They said they were paid lower salaries and were offered fewer benefits because they are Mexicans. They say they were paid $350 to $500 a week and did not get overtime pay. This is the first time illegal aliens have sued. Do you think they have a chance of winning?

3. The U.S. government is offering $1 billion to hospitals that provide emergency care to illegal aliens. For years, hospitals said that the U.S. government was responsible for immigration policy and should pay for the costs of illegal immigrants because it had created the problem. Hospital employees, however, see problems because the government wants them to ask patients questions such as (1) "Are you a legal immigrant with a valid green card?" and (2) "What kind of visa do you have?" What problems do you think these questions can cause?

4. Lawmakers in one state want to allow 400 children of illegal aliens to qualify for in-state tuition at local state colleges and universities. Lawmakers argue that it is not right to punish students who might have been brought here illegally when they were children. This would apply only to students who have lived in the state for three years, graduated from a high school in that state, and filed an affidavit saying they were beginning the process of becoming citizens. Is this a good idea?

Writing ✳

What is your opinion about illegal immigrants? Write a short paragraph.

International Students on American Campuses

Introduction ✳

full text on page 149 (cd track 39)

In the 2011–2012 academic year, the number of international students in U.S. colleges and universities grew almost 6%, to a total of 764,495. Of the top 25 campuses with the most international students, 12 of them have increased international enrollment more than 40% in just five years. Most of these students are attending large public universities in Midwestern states such as Minnesota, Michigan, Indiana, Ohio, and Illinois. The private University of Southern California, with about 10,000 international students, leads all schools.

Vocabulary and Pronunciation ✳

1. **financial aid** - loans and grants that students receive to pay for the costs of education
2. **tuition** - the cost of taking courses for academic credit
3. **a private university** - a school that a private group runs, not the government
4. **a public university** - a school that the government runs

Dictogloss Dictation ✣

Listen to each sentence only once and write down the words you can remember. With a partner, try to reconstruct the entire sentence and write it below as accurately as possible.

1. _____

2. _____

3. _____

Listening for Statistics ✤

Listen and write the number you hear in the chart.

Country	Total	% of international students	1-year % change
COUNTRIES SENDING THE MOST STUDENTS TO THE UNITED STATES IN 2011–2012			
China	194,029		
India			-3.5%
South Korea	72,295		
Saudi Arabia			50.4%
Canada			

Discussion ✳ *With a partner, talk about these questions. Then share your ideas with the class.*

1. Countries like China used to send many more graduate students than undergraduates. Now most are undergraduates. Why do you think this is changing?

2. The number of undergraduate students from Saudi Arabia has increased a great deal. Do you know why they are coming here in such large numbers?

3. Many international students stay in the U.S. after they graduate. Why?

4. Why do international students pay full out-of-state tuition at public universities?

5. What do you think are the most popular majors for international students?

Writing ✳

After your discussion of the five topics above, choose one and write about your experiences here in the United States.

Apolo Ohno

full text on page 150 (cd track 40)

Introduction ✳

Apolo Ohno is the most decorated winter Olympian. He advises people with specific long-term goals to try to enjoy the process. He tells them to have short-term goals and take small steps to reach their final goal.

Vocabulary and Pronunciation ✳

1. **Caucasian** - a racial term applied to Indo-European origin
2. **most decorated** - won the most medals
3. **Olympian** - an athlete who competes in the Olympics
4. **to qualify** - to have the skill or knowledge to do a certain job
5. **ups and downs** - good times and bad times

Pre-Listening Exercise ✦

Work with a partner and read the sentences that describe Apolo Ohno from the time he was born until he became famous for two different achievements. Put the sentences in chronological or logical order from 1 to 9.

_____   From that time on, Ohno had an Olympic dream.

_____   He is also famous for competing and winning in *Dancing with the Stars*, a TV reality

show, in 2007.

___*1*___   After Ohno's Caucasian mother and Japanese father divorced when he was a baby, he

lived with his father.

_____   In 2002 he won his first Olympic medals in speed skating.

_____   When he was six, his father enrolled him in swimming lessons and inline speed skating

lessons.

_____   By the 2010 Olympics, he had won the most Olympic medals (8) of any winter athlete.

_____   After he watched the Winter Olympics in Lillehammer when he was 12 in 1994, he

became interested in short-track speed ice skating.

_____   He had his ups and downs. For instance, in 1998 he finished last in the Olympic trials

and did not qualify for the Olympics.

_____   At thirteen he was the youngest skater admitted to the Olympic Training Center in Lake

Placid, New York.

Dictogloss ✛

Listen to each sentence only once and write down the words you can remember. With a partner, try to reconstruct the sentences in writing as accurately as possible.

1. _____

2. _____

3. _____

4. _____

5. _____

Discussion ✛ *With a partner, discuss the following questions.*

1. Have you ever seen Apolo Ohno on TV?
2. Do you play or have you ever played any sports?
3. Do you like to dance? What kind of dancing do you enjoy?
4. Apolo Ohno had a goal from the time he was twelve. Do you have a goal?
   What will you do to achieve it?

Writing ❖ *Write about one of the following topics.*

1. Write about a goal you have and what steps you will take to achieve it.
2. Write about a sport that you do now or did in the past.
3. Do you enjoy watching great athletes perform? What kinds of sports do you enjoy watching? Why?

Fun with Numbers

full text on page 151 (cd track 41)

Introduction/Vocabulary/Pronunciation ✳

Practice the pronunciation of these words with your teacher.

1. add

2. subtract

3. circle

4. triangle

5. line

6. horizontal line

7. vertical line

8. parallel lines

9. lines in a row   or

10. above, over _____ ★ _____ the line

11. below, under ☾ the line

12. middle, center

Partial Dictation ✳

Listen and fill in the blanks. Then follow the instructions.

1. Draw _____ horizontal lines in a row. Write _____ on the first line. Write _____ on the last line. _____ the two numbers together. Write your answer on the _____ line.

2. Draw a _____ line. To the left of it, write _____. To the right of it, write _____. Subtract the smaller number from the _____ number and write your answer _____ the vertical line.

3. Draw _____ triangles. Next to them draw a _____ In the first triangle write _____. In the _____ _____ write _____. Add the two _____ together and put your answer in the circle.

Dictogloss ✛

Listen to each complete sentence only once and write down the words you can remember. With a partner, try to reconstruct the sentences and write them below. Then do the problems.

1. _____

2. _____

3. _____

4. _____

Discussion ✛ *With a partner, discuss the following.*

1. Do you like math?
2. Are you a good math student?
3. Using the vocabulary in this lesson, design a problem for your partner and have your partner design one for you.

Writing ❖

Write a dictation like the ones in the partial dictation. Make a copy or copies of it.
Have your partner or several people do the dictation and the problem.

Proverbs
(Partial Dictation)

dictation page 1 (cd track 1)

1. There's no **place like home**.

2. Don't **count your chickens** before they're hatched.

3. First **come, first served**.

4. Love makes the world **go 'round**.

5. **Time** is **money.**

6. **Too many cooks** spoil the broth.

7. You can't **teach an old dog** new tricks.

8. You can't have your cake and **eat it too**.

9. **Live** and **learn.**

10. The **early bird** catches the worm.

11. The **first step** is the hardest.

12. The apple doesn't **fall very far** from the tree.

Optimists and Pessimists
(Partial Dictation)

dictation page 4 (cd track 2)

1. The food at McDonald's **isn't very good.**

2. **English grammar** is illogical.

3. There are **so many immigrants** in the U.S.

4. It's been raining for **six straight days.**

5. American cars **are gas guzzlers.**

6. I have to pay a lot **for medical insurance.**

7. My parents **are too strict.**

Brain Teasers
(Partial Dictation)

dictation page 8 (cd track 3)

1. Which is heavier, a pound of feathers, or a **pound of cement**? **(they weigh the same)**

2. How many **birth days** does the average person have? **(one)**

3. Can a man **who is living** in northern United States be buried in Canada?
   (no, he's still living – alive)

4. A little girl is playing **at the beach**. She is making sand piles. She has **three piles** in one
   place and **four piles** in another place. If she puts them **all together,** how many sand piles
   will she have? **(one)**

5. Bob **is standing behind** Sam. Sam is standing behind Bob at the **same time.** How is that
   possible? **(They are standing back to back.)**

6. **Would you rather** have a lion attack *you* or a tiger? **(You have to read this with the
   emphasis on the word "you" so that your answer would be, "I'd rather have the lion
   attack the tiger.")**

7. What word, if pronounced right, **is wrong**, but if pronounced wrong **is right**? **(wrong)**

8. Do you know the thing that has keys that open **no doors,** has space but **no room**, and allows
   you to enter but **not go in**? **(a keyboard)**

Riddle answers: 1. C; 2. D; 3. B; 4. A
Note: This is a fun activity to do after a "real" test. It's a good way to release tension!

Trivia Contest
(Partial Dictation)

dictation page 10 (cd track 4)

1. What does the abbreviation ET **stand for?** (extra terrestrial)

2. What do people put **French, Russian,** and **Italian** dressing on? (salads)

3. What is the **greatest number of babies** that a woman has had at one time? (8)

4. What do people in the United States have to do **on April 15**? (file and pay income tax)

5. What is the name of the **traditional woman's dress** in India? (sari)

6. What do you do when you **grab a bite**? (You get something to eat.)

7. Who wrote **A Christmas Carol**? (Charles Dickens)

8. What sports event takes place **on a diamond?** (baseball)

9. Which is the **largest continent**? (Asia)

10. What **language** do they speak in **Brazil**? (Portuguese)

11. What is present in **tea, coffee, soda,** and chocolate? (caffeine)

12. What was the **first American college** and where **is it located?** (Harvard, Cambridge, MA)

13. Who does a car with the **initials MD** on the license plate **belong to**? (a doctor)

14. Who was both **deaf** and **blind,** but became a **writer**? (Helen Keller)

Cooperative Learning Answers

Set 1: **January, sandwiches, diamond, ear, Shakespeare**

Set 2: **soccer, interesting (exciting), alligator, Chinese, ice cream**

Set 3: **ten, carbonated drinks, Bible, electronic mail, approximately one-half million**

Set 4: **cockroach, money, unidentified flying object, Siam, thirteen**

Chocoholics, Unite!
(Partial Dictation)

dictation page 13 (cd track 5)

Op. 1. Chocolate from Belgium **is the best.**

Fact 2. People crave chocolate more than **any other food.**

Fact 3. Chocolate **consists of chemicals** associated with mood, emotion, and addiction.

Op 4. Chocolate is sinful because it has lots of **fat and calories.**

Fact 5. Chocolate lovers **have been around** for almost 3000 years.

Fact 6. Chocolate comes from cacao beans, and **in ancient times** was used as a form of currency.

Fact 7. **You can find** cacao trees in Africa, Southeast Asia, and in South and Central America.

Op 8. You can **enjoy chocolate more** when you are depressed or stressed.

Note to teachers: This works well when you give students some chocolate before or after the lesson!

What Do You Eat?
(Partial Dictation)

dictation page 16 (cd track 6)

Breakfast. During the work week, <u>**two-thirds**</u> of Americans eat breakfast, <u>**three-fourths**</u> of them at home. About <u>**one in five**</u> eats breakfast at work: <u>**one in ten**</u> while driving or commuting. The most popular breakfast is <u>**hot or cold**</u> cereal (67%), followed by <u>**toast**</u>, or muffins, or bagels (<u>**55 %**</u>), and eggs (<u>**31 %**</u>). <u>**Two-thirds**</u> also snack on cereal, and <u>**29 %**</u> admit they eat cereal for dinner...sometimes.

Weekends. On <u>**Saturday**</u> and Sunday, <u>**87 %**</u> of us eat breakfast at home. Eggs are the <u>**favorite**</u> Sunday breakfast for more than <u>**half**</u>. Bacon, ham, or sausages are nearly as <u>**popular**</u>; so are pancakes or waffles.

Lunch. Sandwiches <u>**are popular**</u> at midday. <u>**Seven**</u> in <u>**ten**</u> of us put our food between two <u>**slices**</u> of bread. <u>**One in three**</u> eats <u>**fast food**</u>.

Dinner. About <u>**eight in ten**</u> who bring home <u>**takeout**</u> food said they prefer everything ready-to-eat, rather than also having a side dish prepared at home. <u>**Pizza**</u> is the favorite food-to-go (the choice of <u>**79 %**</u>), followed by <u>**Chinese**</u> food (<u>**51 %**</u>) and <u>**fast food**</u> such as hamburgers or tacos (<u>**40 %**</u>).

Snacks. Evening is <u>**prime time**</u> for snackers. Nearly <u>**two-thirds**</u> of Americans snack after dinner (<u>**usually**</u> in front of the <u>**TV**</u>), and <u>**15 %**</u> nibble all day long.

The Noblest of Professions
(Partial Dictation)

dictation page 19 (cd track 7)

1. A teacher is a guide in the **adventure of learning**.

2. A teacher is a **salesperson**. The product is **knowledge**.

3. A teacher is a **counselor**, a **nurse**, and a healer of broken hearts.

4. A teacher is **so much more** than what a test can measure.

5. A teacher is a coach, a cheerleader, **and a peacemaker**.

6. A teacher is a psychiatrist fostering **self-esteem** and an optometrist helping students **see clearly**.

7. A teacher is an **actor**, a **comedian**, and a storyteller.

8. A teacher is an X-ray technician **reading minds**, a publisher at the copy machine, and a partner **with parents** in the adventure of education.

Well-paid rankings (these vary from year to year)
1-airline pilot
2-surgeon
3-criminal lawyer
4-electrical engineer
5-electricians, plumbers, and mail carriers all make about the same (no university degree necessary)
6-registered nurse
7-psychologist

The ten most dangerous jobs in U.S. (fatalities per 100,000 in 2011 from U.S. Bureau of Labor Statistics)

1. fishermen (127.3/100,000)
2. logging workers (104)
3. aircraft pilots/flight engineers (56.1)
4. trash/recyclable collectors (36.4)
5. roofers (34.1)
6. structural iron and steel workers (30.3)
7. construction laborers (26.8)
8. farmers/ranchers (26.1)
9. truck drivers (25.9)
10. natural resources workers/miners (22.1)

Dear Mom and Dad
(Partial Dictation)

dictation page 22 (cd track 8)

Dear Mom and Dad,

Since I left for college, I **have been** very bad about writing, and I am sorry for my thoughtlessness in not **having** written before. I will bring you up to date now, but before you read on, please sit down. You are not to read any further unless you are sitting down. OK?

Well then, I am getting along pretty well now. The skull fracture and the concussion I got when I **jumped** out of the window of my dormitory when it **caught** on fire is pretty well **healed** now. I only **spent** two weeks in the hospital, and now I can see almost normally and only **get** these sick headaches once a day. Fortunately, the fire in my dormitory and my jump **were seen** by an attendant at the gas station near the dorm, and he was the one who **called** the fire department and the ambulance. He also **visited** me in the hospital, **brought me** flowers, and since then we **have fallen** in love. We are **about to** marry, and I **am** leaving the university in order to find a job. He is **divorced** and has three young children that he **must support**. This is difficult **to do** on a gas station attendant's salary, and I **must help**.

Correct Verb Tenses *(not on CD)*

I know that you will welcome him into our family with open arms. He is kind, and although not well educated he is ambitious. Although he is of a different race and religion than ours, I know you will not be be bothered by that.

Now that I have brought you up to date, I want to tell you that there was no dormitory fire. I did not have a concussion or skull fracture. I was not in the hospital and there is no boyfriend in my life. However, I am getting a D in history and F in science, and I want you to see those marks in their proper perspective.

Your loving daughter,

Susan

Thanksgiving
(Partial Dictation)

dictation page 26 (cd track 9)

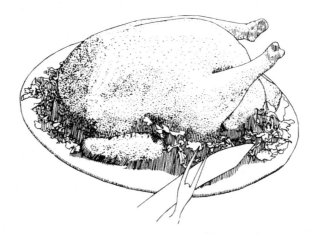

Fact 1. Thanksgiving always comes on the **fourth Thursday** in November.

Op. 2. It is the **most loved** American holiday.

Fact 3. Many people have a big dinner that includes **turkey** and **pumpkin pie**.

Op. 4. Turkey is tastier **than** chicken.

Op. 5. Thanksgiving dinners are **a lot of work** to prepare.

Fact 6. The Pilgrims started this tradition of **giving thanks** in 1621.

Fact 7. They came to Plymouth, Massachusetts, in 1620 to find **religious freedom**.

Fact 8. They came **in the winter** and didn't have enough food to eat.

Fact 9. **The Indians** helped them by giving them food and showing them how **to farm**.

Fact 10. At the end of their first year in America, the Pilgrims **invited the** Indians to celebrate with a **big dinner** in appreciation for their help in surviving their first year.

Fact 11. Thanksgiving is **the busiest** travel holiday of the year. Airports are **crowded**.

We Shall Overcome
(Partial Dictation)

dictation page 28 (cd track 10)

We shall overcome	Deep in my heart
We shall overcome	I do believe
We shall overcome some day.	We shall overcome some day.

Although President Abraham Lincoln's Emancipation Proclamation set the slaves free during **the Civil War** in 1865, blacks **in the 1950's**, especially in the South, still suffered from unfair treatment because of **their race**. Some states did not allow blacks **to vote**. Schools, buses, trains, and public businesses like theaters and restaurants were segregated — separated into facilities for **blacks and whites**.

Imagine being a **black man**, **woman**, or child in 1950 in Mississippi. You **could not vote**. You could go to school with black children only. You could drink only from a separate water fountain, use separate bathrooms, swim in a separate swimming pool, and ride at the **back of the bus**.

In the 40s and 50s, Presidents Roosevelt and Truman had said that discrimination based on race and religion was against the ideals of **American democracy**. However, it was not until 1954 that the Supreme Court said, "Separate educational facilities are inherently unequal." With this ruling, the Civil Rights Movement **was born**. The courts ordered schools to be desegregated.

Now blacks had government support in their fight for equality, and the Civil Rights Movement **had begun**. It took ten years before the Civil Rights Act was passed by Congress. During that time many black citizens were holding peaceful marches and sit-ins **in order to** get voting rights and desegregated schools. They were often violently attacked by whites and even policemen armed with batons, bullwhips, fire hoses, **and dogs**. But still they marched peacefully, singing "We Shall Overcome" while the world watched **on television**.

The song "We Shall Overcome," **adapted from** a black gospel song, became the song of the **Civil Rights** Movement. It was sung during the sit-ins, voter registration drives, and protest marches of those heroic days. Since that time this song **has been sung** by people **all over** the world who are fighting for equality or **for freedom**.

Note to Teachers: This lesson can be used at any time, but it is particularly appropriate before Martin Luther King, Jr. Day in January. It is most effective if the teacher plays/ teaches the song, and students sing it.

Lacrosse
(Partial Dictation)

dictation page 31 (cd track 11)

Answers to chronology in Introduction: 5, 1, 6, 2, 3, 7, 4

Lacrosse was first played centuries ago by North American Indians in preparation for war.

Lacrosse games evolved in Ontario, Canada, and in the U.S. in the 1600's.

Those earliest games had as many as 1,000 players per side, from the same or different tribes.

French-Canadian dentist George Beers standardized the game in 1867 with a new set of rules.

Men's and women's lacrosse were played under the same rules until the mid-1930's.

Women's lacrosse in the U.S. was formed in 1926 at a school in Maryland.

Lacrosse is currently a national sport with more than 250,000 active players.

F   1. Lacrosse is played **with a stick**, the crosse, and the players need to know how to **throw**, **catch**, and scoop.

F   2. Lacrosse is a fast-paced sport and **full of action**.

O   3. **Women are better players** than men because they are more agile.

F   4. Most lacrosse players play for **love of the sport** rather than for financial reward.

O   5. Women's lacrosse is the best sport **on the planet**.

O   6. Lacrosse is **a violent sport**.

F   7. Professional lacrosse in the U.S. has different rules and **is played indoors**.

Buying a Used Car
(Partial Dictation)

dictation page 33 (cd track 12)

Ashvin, age 19, came from India ten years ago with his family and has been driving for one year. He is a university student on a full scholarship. He has a part-time job on weekends in his family's jewelry store. His part-time salary is $150 a week. His parents will co-sign the loan; otherwise, he wouldn't pass bank qualifications. He lives with his family and they pay all of his expenses. The used car he wants to buy is $5800. The down payment is $1160 and the interest rate is 14% because he has no credit record. The monthly payment will be $150 and his car insurance will be $200 a month because of his age and short driving record.

Shu Min, age 24, has just graduated with a master's degree in chemistry. She came to the U.S. six years ago from China and has been a student ever since. She just received her driver's license last year. She has recently accepted a job ($80,000 a year) outside of Dallas and needs a car to get to work. During college years, she worked as a teaching assistant to help pay her tuition. The car she wants is $8,000. The down payment of 20% is $1,600. The loan is for $6,400. Because she has no credit record in the U.S., the bank will require a higher interest rate — 14%. Her monthly payment on this car will be about $600. She will also have to pay $300 a month for car insurance. She can afford it. What if she wants to pay cash? Would you recommend it?

Top 5 car companies in 2012:

> 1. Toyota (world's largest)
> 2. General Motors
> 3. Volkswagen Group
> 4. Hyundai (fastest growing)
> 5. Ford
> > Nissan is # 6
> > Honda is # 7

Top three: Toyota, Honda, General Motors.
Best selling car (sedan) in U.S.: Toyota Camry
Others: Nissan Altima, Ford Fusion, Honda Accord

Bullies
(Partial Dictation)

dictation page 36 (cd track 13)

1. Some bullies are **looking for attention**. *(T)*

2. Most bullies **don't understand** or care about the **feelings of** others. *(T)*

3. Bullies often **pick on** someone they think they have **power over**. *(T)*

4. Most bullies are **high school students**. *(F - most are middle school students)*

5. **Bullying** can make a school a place **of fear** and can lead to **more violence**. *(T)*

6. Kids who are bullies cannot learn to **change their behavior**.

   (F - they need to see a counselor.)

7. **If someone is bullying you**, it's important to tell an adult you can trust. *(T)*

The First Americans
(Partial Dictation)

dictation page 40 (cd track 14)

Archeologists believe Native Americans (Indians) **came from** Asia 25,000 years ago. By the year 5,000 B.C., many different groups lived **in all parts** of North America. Because Indians **lived in** scattered groups and had little contact **with each other**, they developed different cultures. They spoke **over 1000** different languages, wore different types of clothing, built different types **of homes**, and made their living **in different ways**. Those who settled in the northern areas **hunted and fished**. Those who settled in the east and southwest **farmed**. Despite their many differences, **most Indians** shared the belief that people should live in harmony **with nature**. They believed that people should not own land because the land, like the air, stars, and water, **belonged to everyone**. The European settlers **believed in** the ownership of private property. These two very different **ways of life** were the basis of the many conflicts between the Indians and the settlers.

In the early years of discovery and exploration between **1492** and the mid–**1600's**, relations with the Indians were, for the most part, **friendly**. But as more and more settlers arrived, conflicts developed. Indian tribal leaders **were worried** and angry because settlers were crowding people **off their land**. When Indians "sold" land to the settlers, the Indians **misunderstood and thought** they were only giving whites the right **to use the land**.

Many settlers tried to understand the Indian way of life and treat them **fairly**. But others **cheated them** and took their land. While Indians always fought **for their rights**, they were unable to stop the advance of thousands of settlers supported by the **U.S. Army**. Indians won some battles, but they always ended up **losing their lands**.

By 1880, fighting **had stopped**. Finally, the government moved almost all the remaining Indians onto **reservations**. Today, however, less **than half** of the Indians live on reservations. Those who do, try to preserve their tribal **customs** and ways of life. But discrimination by non-Indians, an unwillingness by Indians to **adopt new ways**, and a basic **distrust of** the federal government, have kept many Indians out of the mainstream of **modern life**.

Save Our Planet Award
(Partial Dictation)

dictation page 43 (cd track 15)

1. *The Teen Team.* This **group of students** from Greenland Middle School saw a TV show about how plastic trash on beaches and **in the ocean** kills a million sea birds and fish every year. They organized a group of 15 student volunteers to **collect bottles**, plastic bags, and plastic containers from their city's beaches every month. This has **saved the lives** of many birds and fish.

2. *Erin Brockton.* Erin and her children discovered that **a paper company** in Greenland had been dumping poisonous chemicals in an **empty yard** near her neighborhood. Some of the poison had leaked into the reservoir where the town gets its **drinking water**. Many people got sick. After months of **complaining**, Erin forced the paper company to find other, safer ways **to get rid of** the waste.

3. *VFR (Volunteers for Recycling).* These people spend a lot of time at **the city dump**. Why? Because they want to help Greenland residents **recycle their newspapers**, bottles, and cans. They also organized a "swap shop" at the dump where people could leave **old but good chairs**, TVs, computers, and other **useful things**. Then, people who need them can get them free. Their work has saved the town **thousands of dollars**.

Privacy
(Partial Dictation)

dictation page 46 (cd track 16)

Operator:	Thank you for calling Pizza Castle.
Customer:	Hello, can I order....
Operator:	Can I have your multi-purpose **card number** first, sir?
Customer:	Hold on . . . 123-12-**5889**.
Operator:	Okay. **You're** Mr. Saxe and **you're calling** from 26 Rose Lane. Your home number is 627-734-**5266**. Your office number is **627**-373-5716 and your cell **phone** is 627-266-**2566**. Would you like to have this delivery made to 26 Rose Lane?
Customer:	How **did you get** all my phone numbers?
Operator:	We are connected to the system, sir.
Customer:	**May I order** your Seafood Pizza?
Operator:	That's not **a good idea**, sir.
Customer:	How come?
Operator:	According to **your medical records**, you have high blood pressure and you're overweight.
Customer:	This is crazy! **I want three** Seafood Pizzas.
Operator:	That should be enough for **your family of ten**. The **total is** $49.99, sir, and would you please pay **in cash**? We see that **your credit card** is over the limit.
Customer:	I give up. You know everything **about me**.

Listening Text

Waitress:	Good afternoon. My name is Lily. I am your waitress. Do you know what you want?
Man:	Yes, I'm going to have a grilled cheese and tomato sandwich and coffee.
Waitress:	Good. What kind of cheese do you want? We have Swiss, cheddar, American, and Havarti.
Man:	I'll have plain American cheese.
Waitress:	What kind of bread would you like? We have wheat, light rye, dark rye, multigrain, and white.
Man:	I'll have plain white bread.
Waitress:	What kind of coffee would you like? We have espresso, lattes, cappuccinos, and American coffee.
Man:	I'll have plain American coffee.
Waitress:	That's fine, sir.
Man:	Thank you. Now I'll just sit and read my plain old newspaper.

Answers: b d a c d b

Chicago

What Am I? An American?

(Partial Dictation)   dictation page 48 (cd track 17)

For those of you first-generation children whose parents **were born in another country**, let me tell you that, if you are confused, you are not alone! When I was a teenager, I thought I was the only one **who felt confused**. I asked myself, "**Am I Chinese? or American**?" Young people who have read my book, *The Joy Luck Club*, tell me, "**I feel as though** you've written my life. . . . I'm the only kid in **an all-white community** in all-white American schools. **And I don't know** if I'm Chinese or not. What should I be?" When Amy was 35, she **had a chance to go back** to the country of her parents. She found out, **not how Chinese she was**; she found out how American she was. **Now she knows**!

Made. . . Where?
(Pair Dictation)

dictation pages 51-52 (cd track 18)

Bill Smith started the day early. He set his alarm clock (made in Japan) for six o'clock a.m. While his coffeepot (made in China) was perking, he shaved with his electric razor (made in Hong Kong). He put on a dress shirt (made in Sri Lanka), designer jeans (made in Singapore), and tennis shoes (made in Korea).

After he cooked his breakfast in his new electric fryer (made in India), he sat down with his calculator (made in Mexico) to see how much he could spend today.

After he set his watch (made in Taiwan) to the radio (made in India), he got in his car (made in Germany) and continued his search for a good-paying American job. At the end of yet another discouraging and fruitless day, Bill decided to relax for a while. He put on his sandals (made in Brazil), poured himself a glass of wine (made in France), and turned on the TV (made in Indonesia), and then wondered why he couldn't find a good-paying job in America!

How Honest Are You?
(Pair Dictation)

dictation pages 54-55 (cd track 19)

Note: Tell the students to write out the figures in millions: thirty-three, not 33. They should also use the % sign, not write it out.

According to an article in *The New York Times* on January 8, 2004, titled "Never Lost But Found Daily: Japanese Honesty," if you lost a $100 bill in Tokyo, there is a good chance that it would be returned, and you could claim it.

In Tokyo, with eight million people in the city and thirty-three million in the metropolitan area, a $100 bill would probably find its way to the Tokyo Metropolitan Police Lost and Found Center.

In 2002, people found and brought to the Tokyo Center twenty-three million in cash. 72% of it was returned to the owners once they had persuaded the police it was theirs. About 19% went to the finders after no one claimed the money for half a year.

Children are taught from early on to hand in anything they find to the police in their neighborhood.

The most frequently lost item is umbrellas, 360,000 in 2002. The item with the highest rate of return is the cell phone, 75%.

Do people in your city return things they find? Do you?

What's So Funny?
(Pair Dictation)

dictation pages 58-59 (cd track 20)

Joke 1: "Those people upstairs are very annoying," complained the tenant. "Last night they stomped and banged on the floor until midnight." "Did they wake you?" asked the landlord. "No," replied the tenant. "Luckily, I was playing my tuba."

Joke 2: As a senior citizen was driving down the highway, his car phone rang. Answering, he heard his wife's voice urgently warning him. "Herman, I just heard on the news that there's a car going the wrong way on Route 280. I know you usually take Route 280, so please be careful!" "Yikes," yelled Herman, "it's not just ONE car. It's hundreds of them!"

Eat that Insect?
(Pair Dictation)

dictation pages 61-62 (cd track 21)

Ladybugs are cute and butterflies are pretty, but most people who come face to face with an insect have one thought: Step on it! David Gordon takes a different approach. He cooks bugs and eats them. He thinks insects are a valuable, underused, and delicious source of nutrition. "If you're eating hot dogs, you're eating stuff that's way weirder than a grasshopper," said Gordon as he demonstrated his cooking skills in an elementary school cafeteria. On his grill he prepared grasshopper kebabs, fried crickets, and grilled mealworms. School rules prevented the children from eating bugs, but teachers tried them and thought they were tasty! But beware! Not all bugs taste good, and some are poisonous, especially caterpillars. Even birds and other animals do not want to eat them, which is why some caterpillars can eat and destroy thousands of trees each year.

Underage Drinking

Introduction ❊

dictation pages 64-65 (cd track 22)

1. The legal drinking age in this state is 21. **True: The legal drinking age in all 50 states is 21.**
2. The legal driving age in this state is 17. **False**
3. The cost of car insurance is higher for people under 25 years of age. **True**
4. In the U.S., motor vehicle accidents account for nearly 30% of all deaths among people aged 15 to 24. **True**

(Pair Dictation)

Dear Deena,

I am 17, and though I feel I am an adult, I can't afford to buy my own car, so I must use my parents'. They are good about lending it to me but are absolutely fanatic on the subject of drinking and driving. I know that drinking causes many accidents, but I also know that I can drive safely after drinking only two beers. How can I persuade my parents to see that it's OK?

George from Georgetown

(Students should point out that he's underage and that alcohol slows reaction time and gives one a false sense of invulnerability.)

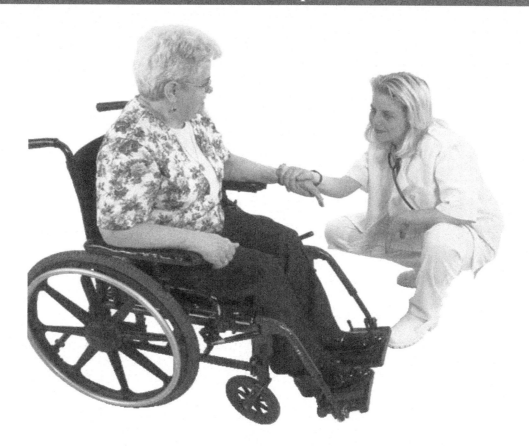

I've Always Wanted to Be a Nurse
(Pair Dictation)

dictation pages 66-67 (cd track 23)

I've wanted to be a nurse since I was a little girl. I used to put bandages on my dolls. I know that nursing isn't for everyone, but every day I feel like I'm making a difference. It's great to see someone get well.

However, it can be very stressful at times. Also I've often had to work nights, weekends, and holidays.

But I've been a nurse for 25 years. I've loved working in pediatrics and surgery. I can't see myself doing anything else.

Kimchi
(Pair Dictation)

dictation pages 69-70 (cd track 24)

It is just fermented cabbage, garlic, and chili peppers, but Asians buy large amounts of kimchi, hoping Korea's national dish is really a wonder drug.

Southeast Asians are stocking up on it. It's very popular in China. And South Koreans, who eat it with every meal, are buying more than usual, hoping its healing powers will make it famous.

"I can't imagine a meal without it," said a housewife. "I'm making my children eat a lot more of it. I certainly believe that they are healthy because they eat a lot of kimchi."

A Korean scientist says this theory may be difficult to prove, but that doesn't mean it doesn't work.

Subway Manners
(Pair Dictation)

dictation pages 72-73 (cd track 25)

1. Do you read a newspaper on the train? Keep it in your own space. Take it with you when you leave.
2. Turn your cell phone off. No one wants to listen to your one-sided conversation.
3. Don't eat smelly, messy, or sticky foods on a train or bus.
4. Don't stare at other passengers.
5. Offer your seat to people with disabilities, elderly people, and pregnant women.

The Top Six and the Top Three
(Pair Dictation)

dictation pages 74-75 (cd track 26)

This is from an informal poll. *Accept other answers that you think are right.*

1. What are the six most common excuses for not handing in your homework?
   Top three: My dog ate it. I was sick. I lost it.

2. Where can a single woman meet an intelligent man?
   Top three: in a museum, a coffee shop, a bookstore

3. What are the favorite American desserts?
   Top three: apple pie, ice cream, brownies

4. What are typical American Sunday dinners?
   Top three: roast beef, baked chicken, pasta

5. Name the reasons why Americans divorce.
   Top three: differences that can't change, adultery, money

6. What are the three most dangerous jobs?
   Top three: fisherman, lumberjack, pilot
   (according to the U.S. Department of Labor Statistics 2011, see page 119)

Possible answers to Cooperative Learning Fun – What would Americans say? Guess! (page 76)

The responses are from an informal survey of Americans and are not to be taken seriously!

Set One

1. Name the best age to marry. **25, 30, 27**
2. Name a sport played with a small ball. *golf, tennis, ping pong*
3. Name two ways Americans can get rich quickly. *lottery, inheritance*
4. Name a very common American last name. *Smith, Johnson, Jones, Brown*
5. Name the three largest American states in size. *Alaska, Texas, California*

Set Two

1. Name four fruits that begin with the letter P. *pear, plum, peach, pineapple*
2. Name a sport that looks easier than it is. *golf, tennis, swimming*
3. Name two organizations that help people in trouble. *Red Cross, Salvation Army*
4. Name a type of bird you hope you never eat. *pigeon, parrot, buzzard*
5. Name a good food to warm you up on a cold night. *soup, chili, hot chocolate*

Set Three

1. Name something you own that was made in a foreign country. *car, clothes*
2. Name a sport that is played in the water. *swimming race, water polo*
3. Name a state many Americans go to for vacation. *Florida, Hawaii, California*
4. Name a word that rhymes with "shake." *cake, bake, make, lake, snake*
5. Name the most famous writer of English/American literature of all time.
   Shakespeare, Mark Twain, Edgar Allan Poe, Agatha Christie

Set Four

1. What's the most you would pay for a movie ticket? *$9.00, $11.00, $15.00, $20.00*
2. Name three U.S. states with large populations.
   California, Texas, New York, Florida, Illinois
3. Name a young and famous singer and actor, female or male.
   Justin Bieber, Ariel Winter, Modern Family, Abigail Breslin, Little Miss Sunshine
4. Name three foods a college student with little money might eat.
   macaroni and cheese, ramen noodles, pizza
5. What's the first thing you do when you get up in the morning?
   take a shower, brush my teeth, get dressed

Opportunity Knocks
(Prediction Dictation)

dictation page 79 (cd track 27)

Most **high** schools will not accept young people who are **over** 17, have a history of school troubles, speak little **English**, or otherwise seem unlikely to be able **to pass** the final exams and graduate in a reasonable amount of **time.** **In** New York, a night **and** day school **was** created for these students.

Four **years** ago, just before his sixteenth **birthday**, Jean-Luc Gerard landed at Kennedy **Airport** with $20.00 in his **pocket**, alone, speaking no **English**, and traumatized by the deaths of his uncle and brother in a West African civil war. **His** mother **was** kidnapped, and he **never** saw her again.

Four **years** later Mr. Gerard **had** graduated from this high school with a full **scholarship** to Dartmouth College. He had been a night student while **working** full-time during the **day**. The teachers helped **him** with tutoring. They **taught** him English. They **helped** him with immigration and gave him a mentor. The mentor even gave him a party when he was **accepted** to college.

More than half of the students at the **school** are recent **immigrants** like Mr. Gerard. Most come to school during the day for intensive **English** classes after they have been turned down by other high schools because of their age. No one at the school has much **money.** Many students at the school hold some kind of **job** to support **themselves**, their children, and sometimes other family **members.**

Overprotected?
(Prediction Dictation)

dictation page 82 (cd track 28)

Dear Amy:

I read you **on** the Internet because I **live** in Europe. I am **married** to a foreigner and **live** in his country. I love it here, but my problem is the difference in attitude about children.

Specifically, I **have** a nine-year-old daughter who must take a bus to the train **station** and then a 20-minute **ride** on a train to get to her school. It is a private bilingual **school**.

Many of the **children** in her **class** come from far **away** on their **own**. In fact, this is quite common in their culture. Children are off to school on their **own** as young **as** kindergarten. I am American and my instinct is not to allow a nine-year-old to go through a big city train **station** on **her own**.

My husband and my daughter's teacher have been pressuring me; she **says** I am overprotective, that I should let my daughter make this trip **by herself**. I am just **not** comfortable with this. Am I overprotective? How can I ever **feel** comfortable about this?

Kate

A Tour of Washington, D.C.
(Prediction Dictation)

dictation page 85 (cd track 29)

Good morning, ladies and **gentlemen**, boys and **girls**. My name is George, and I am your personal tour guide. For the **next** six hours, we **will** be exploring exciting Washington, D.C., the **capital** of the United States. Let's start off with a bang and visit the **White** House, D.C.'s **most** popular tourist attraction. Who knows, **maybe** we'll even get to **see** the President at work in the Oval Office. Then it's only a hop, skip, and a jump to the Smithsonian Institution, where you **could** probably spend a whole week; there's so much to **see**. Then it's on to the Lincoln Memorial. If you ask a hundred Americans who the greatest **President** of the U.S. was, most will say Abraham Lincoln. That's because he signed the Emancipation Proclamation to free the slaves. And here's the Big One! For lunch, we're **going** to the Capitol Building Cafeteria, where you'll get to **meet** famous politicians. You may even ask them to sign their autographs for the low, low, low price of $50. HA! HA! HA! All aboard!

Answers for A Tour of Washington, D.C.

1. John wanted to go to Washington, D.C.
2. Unfortunately, he doesn't know how to drive.
3. And he couldn't afford to fly.
4. So he asked Mary to drive to D.C.
5. She refused to drive to D.C.
6. He begged her to drive to D.C.
7. She finally agreed to drive to D.C.
8. They planned to leave at 2:00 on Friday.
9. On Thursday John's advisor told him to study harder.
10. Mary's professor also advised her to study.
11. They promised to study hard.
12. So they decided not to go to D.C.

International Women's Day
(Prediction Dictation)
dictation page 88 (cd track 30)

International Women's Day **is** a day to honor **and** praise women for their accomplishments. In some **countries**, such as China, Russia, and Zambia, it is an official holiday. In other countries, such as the United States, it is not a **public** holiday, but people celebrate **it**. Some **women**, such as Mother Teresa from Calcutta, India, have received **honors** for their work with the poor. Others, such as Aung San Suu Kyi of Myanmar and Wangari Maathai **from** Kenya, **are** honored for their work to make their **country's** government serve its **people** better. Over the years **some** progress has been made in **many** parts of the world, but women still have a long **way** to go.

Too Much Clutter
(Prediction Dictation)
dictation page 90 (cd track 31)

Dear Dora,

My husband and I **have** been married for thirty-two **years**. It **is** a good marriage. We are **very** happy, **but** there is one problem. Alan **is** a pack rat. He never throws anything **away**. For example, he **reads** two newspapers **every** day and he keeps them around the **house** in case he wants to reread an article. Most of the time **he** never does. He also keeps things like broken watches and old clothes that he **wore** in high **school**.

On the other hand, I usually throw **away** things I will never use again. Sometimes when my husband is out of the **house**, I throw away some **of** his things, and I don't tell him about **it**. I feel a little guilty, but I can't stand so much clutter. What should I do?

Carol

What's the Best Way to Discipline Kids?
(Prediction Dictation)

dictation page 92 (cd track 32)

1. Talk about It!

"To teach **my** children **a** lesson, I prefer **to** talk to them about what **they** did wrong. My two **kids** often misbehave, but they always react better to a conversation than a scolding."   (*Mexico*)

2. Take Away a Privilege

"I prefer to take away **my** children's computer and texting privileges when they **need** to be disciplined. I do this **when** talking doesn't work." (*U.S.*)

3. Send Them to Their Rooms

"You have to discipline **your** kids. But pain can't teach **kids** as much as love can. I send them to **their** rooms." (*China*)

4. Physical Punishment

"Sometimes a spanking **is** necessary. I think it works **for** children ages 5 to 8." (*Russia*)

Toys for Girls, Toys for Boys
(Prediction Dictation)

dictation page 94 (cd track 33)

Recently a thirteen-**year**-old girl wanted **to** give **her** four-year-old brother a gift for Christmas. She wanted to **give** him an "Easy-Bake Oven" because he likes to help **his** mother bake cookies.

There **was** a problem. She looked at the ads. All of the **ovens** were pink or purple, and all of the ads showed little **girls** with the toy ovens.

The girl, McKenna Pope, was upset. Why were toy ovens only for **girls**? She got 40,000 **people** to sign a petition and sent it to the manufacturer, Hasbro, a big toy company. She was successful. Now there **are** also "Easy-Bake Ovens" in blue, silver, and black, and the ads have **boys** playing with the **ovens**, as well.

Pampered Pooches
(Prediction Dictation, Listening) *dictation page 96 (cd track 34)*

Prediction Dictation

What do **you** buy for a person who has everything? That **is** a common question. A new question **is**, what do you **do** for a dog who **has** everything?

Pet spending is **now** over 50 billion **dollars** per year, up from 45 billion **dollars** a few **years** ago. Dogs wear Ralph Lauren cashmere **sweaters**, Burberry raincoats, and diamond collars, and have boxes **of** toys.

93% of dog **owners** consider their **dogs** to be members of **their** family. They enjoy **buying** things for their **dogs**.

Listening Text

There are many good reasons to own a dog. Here are five of them. The first is physical activity. People who own dogs often have better physical health because they need to walk, exercise, and care for their dogs.

A second reason is that dogs may help lower blood pressure. Studies show that during a medical examination when a dog was present people's heart rate and blood pressure were lower.

Another reason is that dogs may help relax a person and reduce everyday stress. Dogs may help us think less about our problems and worries.

In addition, a dog may help us feel less lonely.

The last reason is about elderly people. Elderly people who live alone say that their dog gives them a reason for living.

Check List of What You Heard

_____	1.	You will feel safer if there is a dog in the house.
✓	2.	You will relax more and reduce everyday stress.
✓	3.	You will increase your physical activity because you will have to walk your dog.
✓	4.	A dog will help reduce your heart rate and lower your blood pressure.
_____	5.	A dog can help you adjust to serious illness or death; you can turn to it for comfort.
_____	6.	Families feel happer if they have a dog.
✓	7.	Dogs give elderly people who live alone a reason for living.
✓	8.	A dog makes us feel less lonely.

Little People of America
(Dictogloss, Listening)

dictation page 98 (cd track 35)

Dictogloss Pre-Listening

1. Can I give birth to a dwarf?

2. Do these people have normal intelligence?

3. Are there many people with dwarfism in the U.S.?

Listening Text

R: I understand there are about 1500 people at this conference.

A: Yes. Some of the younger little people come with their parents, who are of average stature.

R: What are the causes of dwarfism?

A: It is a chemical change within a single gene that begins during conception. It is not caused by anything the parents have done during pregnancy or before. Nine out of ten children born with this condition have average-sized parents.

R: Are there different types of dwarfism?

A: Yes, but the most common form is called achondroplasia, which accounts for 70% of all cases.

R: Is dwarfism a disability?

A: We don't want to be considered disabled, although some of us have spinal and orthopedic problems. Most of us have normal intelligence, normal life spans, and reasonably good health.

R: Coming to a conference like this is a great way to socialize with others like yourself.

A: Yeah, it's wonderful because here I can find people who understand the day-to-day things I experience. At least one time a year, I get to feel normal. People here instantly connect and it's like, "wow!" you could actually meet someone for a long-term relationship.

R: What kind of activities are there?

A: There are workshops for our relatives and friends who want to learn more about our condition. Medical specialists provide counseling on topics like neurological concerns, pregnancy, and psychological issues.

R: I see that there are other fun activities as well.

A: Uh, huh. There are fashion shows, dances, soccer games, and typical tourist trips to interesting places.

R: What's the best part for you?

A: The people you meet and exchange e-mails with. I'm definitely going to check out the guy scene! Who knows, I may find someone short, dark, and handsome!

Note: The book, *Little People: Learning to See the World Through My Daughter's Eyes*, by Dan Kennedy; Rodale Publishers, is an excellent chronicle of a father whose daughter is a dwarf. We recommend it!

Check List of What You Heard – Little People of America, *continued*

  ✓   1. What are the causes of dwarfism?

  ✓   2. It's a chemical change within a single gene that begins during conception.

        3. Most dwarfs suffer from ill health.

  ✓   4. Nine out of ten children born with this condition have average-sized parents.

        5. Achondroplasia is a rare form of dwarfism.

  ✓   6. Some of us have spinal and orthopedic problems.

  ✓   7. People here instantly connect, and it's like "wow!".

        8. I met someone, and I'm in a long-term relationship.

  ✓   9. There are workshops for families and friends.

  ✓   10. I'm definitely going to check out the guy scene!

Homeschooling
(Dictogloss and Listening) *dictation pages 100-101 (cd track 36)*

Dictogloss Pre-Listening

1. Why is homeschooling becoming more acceptable?

2. Who probably does most of the teaching at home? Why?

3. What do you think is one disadvantage of homeschooling?

Listening Text

Why did you choose homeschooling for your daughter?

My husband and I were not happy with the education Eve was getting in the public schools, and we didn't want to send her to private school, which is too expensive and too far away. My husband and I believed that we could give Eve a better education at home, a place where she will be excited about learning and be challenged.

Is homeschooling legal?

Yes, it is now, in every state. Back in the 1970's when conservative Christians wanted to homeschool their children for religious reasons, it was not really accepted by mainstream Americans. But in the 1980's and 90's it became more popular, not only for the religious right, but for thousands of parents like ourselves who felt we could do a better job than the public schools.

How does homeschooling work?

When we first started this project, we copied the traditional classroom subjects, trying to improve on them. But we later tried other approaches which worked even better. We can buy lesson plans in all subjects from organizations and schools. We use the Internet for virtual courses offered by different schools, and we have joined a network of families called the HS Club, where we parents share our expertise and have support groups. Sometimes we hire tutors.

Do you and your husband have teaching degrees?

I graduated from a two-year college where I studied English, and my husband has a master's degree in engineering. I do most of the teaching during the day, but we have Eve do a lot of independent study on topics that interest her, and we take lots of field trips to museums.

Were you at all worried that Eve could become isolated from other children her age?

Actually, that was a concern in the beginning, but we have this network of activities that put homeschoolers together. For example, in the HS Club we have a theater group, a problem-solving group, a ski group, and a math club. We also have science fairs and music recitals. We get together often, and Eve has made many friends.

Check List of What You Heard – Homeschooling, *continued*

____✓____ 1. We didn't want to send her to private school.

____✓____ 2. At home she will be excited about learning and be challenged.

_____ 3. Two million children are now homeschooled.

____✓____ 4. In the 1980's and 90's, it became more popular.

____✓____ 5. We can buy lesson plans in all subjects from organizations and schools.

____✓____ 6. We parents share our expertise and have support groups.

_____ 7. All parents of homeschooled children have college degrees.

____✓____ 8. I do most of the teaching during the day.

____✓____ 9. We have this network of activities that put homeschoolers together.

_____ 10. Eve has many friends in her neighborhood.

Discussion answers

A. Fact or Opinion? 1. Fact 2. Opinion 3. Fact 4. Opinion 5. Fact

B. True, False, or IDK (I don't know):

1. IDK 2. IDK 3. False 4. IDK 5. IDK 6. True 7. False 8. IDK

What's in a Name?
(Partial Dictation, Dictogloss)

dictation pages 103-104 (cd track 37)

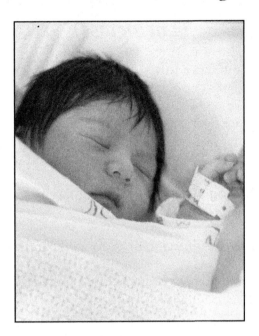

Partial Dictation

Some people name their children after **movie stars** or famous people. In the 1940's many girls **named** Shirley **were named** after a child actress, Shirley Temple. Nowadays we **often meet** children named Celine and Brad.

When people from other **countries** come to the United States, **either** as international students or as **immigrants**, they often change their names and **adopt** English names. They do this **for several** reasons. First, English speakers may have **difficulty** understanding and **pronouncing** their names correctly. Second, people may have **trouble remembering** their names. Third, because they are in a new country, they may want **to change** their lives and begin with a new name.

Dictogloss

1. What is your mother's name?
2. Although his name was Peter, his friends called him Pete.
3. Some famous people, like Madonna, use only one name.
4. If you have a son, what will you name him?
5. If you have a daughter, what will you name her?

Driver's Licenses
for Illegal Immigrants?
(Dictogloss)

dictation page 105 (cd track 38)

Note to teachers: If the students have to listen twice, that's fine!

1. Karen Johnson. No! They are taking jobs away from Americans and legal immigrants.

2. Jason Garcia. Yes! They need to take the test and understand the laws of the road.

3. Helen Chen. No! They should not have the same rights and privileges because they are here without permission.

4. David Peterson. Yes, because they need to drive to work, and they need insurance.

5. Minnie Lee. No! They should go back home because there are too many crazy drivers on the roads anyway.

Fact or Opinion *(see page 106)*

1.	O
2.	F
3.	O
4.	O
5.	F

International Students
on American Campuses
(Dictogloss, Listening)   *full text on pages 107-108 (cd track 39)*

Dictogloss

1. Most international students are attending big public universities in the Midwest.

2. International students do not get financial aid.

3. International students pay full out-of-state tuition at public universities.

Listening for Statistics

COUNTRIES SENDING THE MOST STUDENTS TO THE UNITED STATES IN **2011–2012**			
Country	**Total**	**% of international students**	**1-year % change**
China	194,029	25.4%	23.1%
India	100,270	13.1%	-3.5%
South Korea	72,295	9.5%	-1.4%
Saudi Arabia	34,139	4.5%	50.4%
Canada	26,821	3.5%	-2.6%

Possible Answers for Discussion

1. Many Chinese can now afford to pay the high cost of a U.S. education.
2. The Saudi government gives free scholarships to study in the U.S.
3. Many stay for job opportunities that offer experience and high salaries.
4. They have to pay an out-of-state tuition because their parents are not taxpayers.
5. The most popular majors for international students in no particular order are: computer science, engineering (all types), chemistry, biology, business

Apolo Ohno

dictation pages 109-110 (cd track 40)

Pre-listening: Chronological Order

4 8 1 7 2 9 3 6 5

(Dictogloss)

1. Apolo Ohno was born on May 22 (twenty second), 1982.

2. Apolo was a great winter sports athlete.

3. Apolo was raised in Seattle by his father, who was a hair stylist.

4. Apolo and his dance partner were champions in May, 2007.

5. When he was 12, he decided to become the best speed skater in the world.

Fun with Numbers
(Partial, Dictogloss)

dictation pages 111-112 (cd track 41)

Partial Dictation

1. Draw **5** horizontal lines in a row. Write **25** on the first line. Write **75** on the last line. **Add** the two numbers together. Write your answer on the **middle** line.

   <u>25</u>　　<u>　　</u>　　<u>100</u>　　<u>　　</u>　　<u>75</u>

2. Draw a **vertical** line. To the left of it, write **200**. To the right, write **100**. Subtract the smaller number from the **larger** number and write your answer **below** the vertical line.

3. Draw **2** triangles. Next to them draw a **circle**. In the first triangle, write **70**. In the **second triangle**, write **14**. Add the two **numbers** together and put your answer in the circle.

   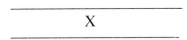

Dictogloss

1. Between two parallel lines, write the letter X.

   _____
   　　　　　　　X
   _____

2. Inside a circle, write the word "mother."

3. Below a triangle, write the number 90.

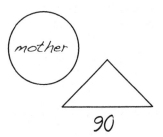

4. Inside a circle, draw a face.

Other Books from Pro Lingua

Three other books of dictations
by Catherine Sadow and Judy DeFilippo

Basic Dictations *(launched-beginner – photocopyable) text and CD*
The topics and vocabulary covered in the book are chosen to help newcomers to the U.S. survive and get around in their new country.

Great Dictations *(high-beginner to low-intermediate) text and CD*

Dictations for Discussion *(intermediate to advanced) text and 2 CD's*
The students are given newspaper or magazine articles in dictations providing varied, high-interest topics of discussion, some follow-up research, and writing practice.

As in **Interactive Dictations**, several dictation techniques are used, all involving filling in blanks in a gapped text. Listening to the articles read by native speakers on CD helps build listening comprehension.

Dictation Riddles *(153* **photocopyable** *riddles – **high-beginner to advanced**) text and 4 CD's*
The students take the riddle in dictation, while trying to guess the person, place, or thing described. Discussion of the riddle and additional background information can follow.

Conversation Strategies   29 structured pair activities for developing strategic conversation skills at the intermediate level. Students learn the words, phrases, and conventions used by native speakers in the active give-and-take of everyday conversation.

Discussion Strategies   Carefully structured pair and small-group work at the high-intermediate level. Excellent preparation for students who will participate in academic or professional work that requires effective participation in discussions and seminars.

In My Opinion   50 contemporary, thought-provoking topics presented in two basic **photocopyable** formats. Just over half of them are in the form of a questionnaire that students fill out and/or respond to orally. Then they compare responses and discuss the "gaps" between their views – what is good/bad, right/wrong, liberal/conservative, and so on. The other activities use opinion cards, 12 to a page, asking the cardholder to voice an opinion to be agreed with or challenged by the others in the class.

Conversation Inspirations   A **photocopyable** collection of over 2400 topics.

Surveys for Conversation   64 one-page **photocopyable** surveys to prompt conversation.

TalkAbouts   72 everyday situations illustrated to prompt conversation. **Photocopyable**.

Faces   50 **photocopyable** drawings of faces invite character invention and conversation.

For more information and sample materials, or to order, visit www.ProLinguaAssociates.com or call 800-366-4775 with questions or to order.